Soul Satisfied

The *un*-Learning of Love Journey

Debra Enile Armand

Debra Enile Armand

All scripture quotations unless otherwise indicated are taken from the Holy Bible, Amplified Version.

ISBN:

Published by:

RedTrini Publishing

Cover design by:

Majid K

Edited by:

Alkins Proofreading & Training Gurus, LLC

www.alkinsgurus.com

CONTENTS

ACKNOWLEDGMENTS

Writing "The *un*-Learning of Love Journey" has been and continues to be an incredible experience, and I could not have done it without the support and encouragement of numerous individuals that are in my life or crossed my path to teach me the life lessons learned.

First and foremost, my deepest gratitude goes to The One Who is Love, God the Father, Jesus Christ my Lord and Savior and His Holy Spirit who continues to teach and transform me every day. Christ is my mentor and guide, whose wisdom and insight have been invaluable every step of the way.

To my sons, Jonathan and Joshua Armand, your unwavering love, support and understanding provided me with the strength and inspiration to pursue my passion. Thank you for always being there to uplift and give me sound advice during challenging times.

I began this journey to learn how to love you, your wives and my grandchildren unconditionally and it has evolved so much more, transforming me in ways beyond my imagination.

A heartfelt thanks to my friends, especially Pauline Rose-Noel, for listening, providing feedback, and being my prayer and sojourning partner during this journey. I deeply appreciate your friendship and support.

I am also grateful to my editor, Claudette Allen, whose keen eye and dedication helped transform my writing into its best form. Your suggestions and patience made this book what it is today.

Special thanks to my family in Trinidad and Tobago who have encouraged and supported me throughout my life.

To the readers of "The *un*-learning of Love Journey," thank you for joining me on this path. Your curiosity and engagement breathe life into these pages.

Finally, a profound thanks to all the unnamed souls who have guided, inspired, and accompanied me along this journey. Each one of you holds a special place in my heart.

INTRODUCTION

In our bustling lives, where the concept of love has been twisted and turned into a version barely recognizable from its true essence, Soul Satisfied: The *un*-Learning of Love Journey emerges as a beacon of hope. This daily devotional book invites you on a sacred journey that ventures deep into the heart of the most profound love you will ever encounter: the unconditional love of God.

Our world is rife with misconceptions about love. We are taught that love is conditional, must be earned, or comes in grand gestures. We chase after fleeting feelings and superficial validations, mistaking them for the love for which we deeply yearn. This misunderstanding leaves us feeling unfulfilled, always searching for something more, something more profound.

Soul Satisfied seeks to dismantle these misconceptions, guiding one through unlearning the distorted beliefs onto which we have held.

Through its pages, explore the biblical truth of God's love — a love so pure, vast, and unfathomable that it defies our earthly perceptions. It is a love that does not ask for anything in return, embraces us in our imperfections, and is steadfast throughout our lives.

Each daily reading in this devotional is designed to inspire and challenge you, gently leading you toward a restorative transformation. As you delve deeper into understanding God's unconditional love, you will find your soul satisfied in ways you never thought possible. You will discover a newfound freedom in love that liberates, heals, and renews.

Let Soul Satisfied: The *un*-Learning of Love Journey be your guide as you embark on this life-changing exploration of Divine love.

Open your heart to the lessons it holds, reflect on the passages, and allow them to reshape your understanding of true love.

Be inspired to live out this love in your life, extending grace, forgiveness, and compassion to reflect the love God has lavished upon you.

Welcome to your journey toward a soul satisfied by the unlearning of love and the relearning of the love that truly matters — the unconditional love of God. Let this journey be of discovery, healing, and deep, abiding joy.

Day 1

Rediscover True Love

Scripture: **Romans 8:35, 38- 39**: "Who shall ever separate us from the love of Christ? Will tribulation, or distress, or persecution, or famine, or nakedness, or danger, or sword?" [38]For I am convinced that neither death nor life, neither angels nor demons, neither the present nor the future, nor any powers, [39]neither height nor depth, nor anything else in all creation, will be able to separate us from the love of God that is in Christ Jesus our Lord."

Devotional:

So many may say, "Yes, I know God loves me." I agree that you know God loves you on an intellectual level. So did I. But my question is, "**Do you truly BELIEVE God loves you?**" Most of my Christian life has been in the "knowing" that God loves me.

I thought I fully believed that until I faced sudden tragic circumstances, like the death of loved ones, life situations that I viewed as unfavorable, divorces, persecutions on the job, betrayals of close friendships, infidelity in marriages, trials, and tribulations. Then I would ask, "God, where are You? Why am I going through this? Why did You allow this to happen to me?" Those questions made me realize that I honestly did not believe God loved me, or at least He did not love me the way I expected or wanted.

This journey you are about to embark upon will challenge you to question your knowledge and belief of God's unconditional love for you and help you redefine the meaning of love while unlearning your beliefs of love. I encourage you to open your hearts and minds to this love relationship that will change you forever.

Reflection:

Today, we embark on a journey of rediscovering true love—the unconditional love of God. It is a love that knows no boundaries, transcends time and space, and remains unwavering in the face of all circumstances. As we delve deeper into this 30-day devotional, let us open our hearts and minds to grasp the enormity of God's love for us. May it permeate every aspect of our lives, transforming our relationships and understanding of what it truly means to love and be loved.

Take a moment to reflect on God's unconditional love through the Bible verses listed above.

Consider how this love has impacted your life and carried you through various seasons. Or, if you have never experienced God's unconditional love, will you open your heart and mind to experience a love that can transform your life for eternity?

As you begin this devotional journey, ask God to reveal more of His love and help you embrace it fully.

Prayer:

Heavenly Father, thank you for the gift of Your unconditional love. Open my heart to experience its depth and magnitude. Help me truly grasp my unbreakable bond with You by accepting Jesus Christ's sacrifice so that I can reunite with You. Teach me to love others with the same selfless and unconditional love You are teaching and showing me.

In Jesus' Name, Amen.

Day 2

Embracing Love's Incomprehensible (an amount, estimate, size, degree, or extent that cannot be fully understood) Measure

Scripture: **Ephesians 3:17-19**: "So that Christ may dwell in your hearts through your faith. And may you, having been [**deeply**] **rooted** and [**securely**] **grounded in love**, [18]be fully capable of comprehending with all the saints (God's people) the width and length and height and depth of His love [fully experiencing that amazing, endless love]; [19]and [that you may come] to know [practically, **through personal experience**] the love of Christ which far surpasses [mere] knowledge [without experience], that you may be filled up [throughout your being] to all the fullness of God [so that you may have the richest experience of God's presence in your lives, completely filled and flooded with God Himself]."

The definition of unconditional love is simply having the best interest of others without wanting anything in return.

Devotional:

It is impossible to comprehend fully the measure of God's love for us. Yet, as followers of Christ, we are called to embrace this boundless love and to allow it to anchor us in our faith. Today, let us meditate on the incomprehensible dimensions of God's love and seek to deepen our understanding of its vastness. We will examine several verses in **1 John 4: 4,8,12,16, Romans 5:8,** and **Deuteronomy 13:3.** Many more amazing scriptures can be studied. As we do so, may we become vessels through which this love flows, reaching out to a world in need.

God's love for us and what our love should be for Him and others is an agape love different from any other type of love.

Agape love denotes goodwill, benevolence, and **willful delight** toward the recipient. It is not based on emotions of romanticism, sexual or brotherly love. The world has portrayed, and unfortunately, we have bought into, that love is a feeling, thereby promoting and selling romance and sex as love. So, we look for a sensation, and when we no longer have that feeling, we say we have fallen out of love, or we search outside of our relationships to capture that "feeling" with someone else.

I remember the first time my then husband proposed the idea to me that love was not a feeling but a decision, I was so offended. I ignorantly thought, at the time, that he was a typical man who was incapable of getting in touch with his emotional side, so he was using that as an excuse. I have since come to learn that he was right.

Agape, unconditional love, whose Source is God, **decides to love** others unselfishly, having their best interest at heart.

17

The love chapter in the Bible, **1Corinthians 13**, tells us about the attributes of unconditional love and who God is.

Reflection:

Take a few moments to envision the vastness of God's love. Picture His love stretching wide, long, high, and deep, surrounding you in every way. Reflect on how this love has touched your life and how it can transform your relationships with others. Allow yourself to receive God's love freshly today.

Prayer:

Loving God, we are in awe of your immeasurable love for us. Help us embrace this love and allow it to penetrate every aspect of our lives. Increase our capacity to love and show us how to extend Your love to those around us.

In Jesus' Name, Amen.

Continue with this devotional, exploring different aspects of God's unconditional love each day and providing space for reflection, prayer, and growth in understanding and experiencing this incredible love.

Day 3

A love That Teaches Me How to Love God, Myself, and Others

Scripture: **Matthew 22:37-40:**

"And Jesus replied to him, 'You shall love the Lord your God with all your heart, and with all your soul, and with all your mind. [38]This is the first and greatest commandment. [39]The second is like it. You shall love your neighbor as yourself (unselfishly seek the best or higher good for others). [40]The whole Law and the (writings of the) Prophets depend on these two commandments.'"

Devotional:

Jesus gave this answer in response to a question asked by a Sadducee, a lawyer (an expert in Mosaic Law) who asked Jesus what the greatest commandment in the Law is.

In **verse 37**, Jesus told him and taught us that the greatest commandment in order of priority is to love the Lord, our God, with all our heart, soul, and mind.

This is our greatest priority on the face of this earth because it is foundational for everything else we build upon.

Learning Who God is and how to love Him genuinely cannot be overstated. We can look around the world today and in our own lives to see the devasting effects of not knowing, embracing, and abiding in this divine Truth. Many have gone astray and formed their gods to suit their lifestyles; there are wars and every kind of evil work being done to humanity because people have rejected the True and Living God.

To know God is to know unconditional love. When you understand this type of love that unselfishly seeks the best interest of others, it will make the world a better place in which to live.

Am I speaking of some utopian existence? No. I am speaking of knowing the God who loves us unconditionally because He is the Source of the love we seek and need so desperately.

We are forever transformed into His image and likeness when we understand, embrace, and abide in His love.

Jesus taught that the second greatest commandment is to love our neighbors (brothers/sisters/co-workers/bosses/cashier in the grocery store, love people) as we love ourselves. Now, this may be easier said than done. For many, to love others seem easier than loving ourselves. We have yet to learn that **we can only love others to the degree we have learned to love ourselves.** To love ourselves, we must be healed from our identity crisis, from the labels given to us by others that we have adopted as our own, that contradict our true and original identity found in Christ.

What is your name? I do not mean the name on your birth certificate or the names you secretly call yourself deep within your heart, nor the names that equate to saying, "I am not good enough; I am not worthy of being loved." Those names.

21

It is vital to become aware of this as we embark upon the journey into the commandment given here. Without knowing who God truly is and who He says we are, we go through life with an identity crisis, always searching, looking, and adopting false personas to feel better about ourselves and to be accepted by others (external validation). As we embrace God's unconditional love, it will heal us of these traumas, and we will emerge to be the men and women God created us to be. We cannot love our neighbors if we do not divinely love ourselves. I purposely said divinely, not narcissistically. We cannot love ourselves until we love God with all our being. To know Him is to love Him.

This process has power because, like the caterpillar that changes into a beautiful butterfly, so too, we are transformed the more we know and love God. This is why it is so important to read the Bible, the Word of God, that gives us glimpses into the character of God.

Nehemiah 9 is one I am reading and slowly digesting now, but there are so many. **No matter what the world may say, you cannot love who you do not know.**

Reflection:

Ask the Lord to show you who you think you are and who He says you are, being honest and transparent before Him. Things left hidden cannot be healed. You cannot heal what you will not reveal.

What is not acknowledged will always be our Achilles heel. If you are unsure because you have worn a mask (to be loved and accepted by others) for so long, ask a trusted friend or loved one to help you here. Begin to commit these scriptures to memory and look through God's Word to discover your true identity.

Genesis 1:26-28	Romans 8:14
Psalms 4:3	Matthew 10:29-31
Ephesians 5:8	Psalms 139:14
Isaiah 44:24	Jeremiah 1:5
Ephesians 1:4	Isaiah 46:4 John 1:48

Debra Enile Armand

Prayer:

Most loving Father, thank you for loving me with a love I may not fully understand but desperately need. You know everything I have been through that has brought me to this point.

Teach me my identity, which is found only in you. Heal me from the inner wounds that have separated me from Your love.

Restore me to my Edenic nature and teach me, each day, to love You and myself the way You do. You know my name, so help me understand it also.

In Jesus' Name. Amen.

Day 4

A Love That Heals

Scripture: **Luke 8:26-39:**

Verse 27: "Now when Jesus stepped out on land, He was met by a man from the city [of Gerasa] who was possessed with demons. For a long time he had worn no clothes, and was not living in a house, but among the tombs."

Devotional:

In these scriptures, we can see the transformative, emotional, and spiritual healing power of unconditional love, of who God is, demonstrated in the personhood of Jesus Christ. Let us think of our current or past state upon or before encountering the love of God. Here is a man who was in a terrible emotional and spiritual state, possessed by demons for a long time (identified later as Legion, for there were many). This made me think of the emotional hurts and trauma that kept me entrapped for most of my life.

The unseen emotional pain that was covered up by years of embracing different masks, both spiritual (the scriptures I would learn and quote but deep down did not know how to believe, becoming religious without an abiding relationship with Christ, going through the motions) and emotional, left me empty within. Secretly and silently over the years, I prayed for deliverance.

This man was in dire need of unconditional love. He wore no clothes and lived in no house but among the tombs (these were probably burial places built above the ground or natural caves in the hillside). Cave tombs often had two chambers, one remaining empty as long as relatives were still alive.

Such tombs frequently were used as shelters by lepers, demoniacs, and the poor. He lived among the dead because he was spiritually dead within, as are so many. From the CEO to the ghetto, so many are living in spiritual and emotional tombs. But we do not have to.

Even in his condition, when he saw Jesus, he cried out to him. That demonstrates that no matter what your condition is, whether you sit at the head of the table at the board meetings or you are physically sitting at the table in prison, you can cry out to God. Though many demonic spirits entrapped this man, he knew this should not be his perpetual state of being. Somewhere within him, he knew he was not created to be enslaved like this. Somewhere within him, he knew this was not who he was created to be. This was not his identity. So, when He saw the One who created him, he cried out to Him for deliverance.

Verse 29 shows how much God/Jesus/Holy Spirit loves us.

The verse said that Jesus was **already commanding the unclean spirit to come out of the man** while he was crying out to Jesus. Christ does the same for us today. He wants to heal us deep within from everything that has kept us bound and in shackles and has prevented us from experiencing His unconditional love.

This reminds me of a song by Tasha Cobbs called "Break Every Chain." For every chain that has held us bound, Christ has come to free us and freed us to experience His love like we never had before.

Verse 30, "Then Jesus asked him, 'What is your name?'" For the powerful transformative emotional healing to occur, we must confess who we think we are and our identity as we see ourselves.

That may be the name somebody called us outside our given name, such as "stupid, dumb, unloved, imbecilic, not pretty enough, not thin enough, not light-skinned enough, uneducated, a sexual vessel to be used by others, no matter what I do it is not good enough, only accepted if you act a certain way, or academically excellent... whatever it was, it conveyed that we are not worthy of being unconditionally loved, just as we are. We all got labeled with an identity that we have carried and showed up as in life.

Jesus knew this man's name.

He wanted the man to know who and what he saw himself as so Christ could show him his true identity. Jesus must break those bonds first for healing to take place and for us to embrace our identity as to who He says we are. Another song by Tasha Cobbs I like to listen to with this teaching is called "You Know My Name."

Genesis 1:26 says, "Then God said, let us (Father, Son, Holy Spirit) make man in Our image, according to Our likeness (not physical, but a spiritual personality and moral likeness)." **Verse 27** says, "So God created man in His own image, in the image and likeness of God He created him, male and female He created them." Imagine you believe that God is unconditional love (which He is). In that case, it is any wonder that unconditional love is the hole in our soul that an imitation or counterfeit version cannot fill. **What is your name? Jeremiah 1:5,7-10** shows us how God sees us. Jeremiah 1:5 is how most of us should see ourselves.

God says, "Before I formed you in the womb, I knew you (approved of you as My chosen instrument), and before you were born, I consecrated you (to Myself as My own); I have appointed you as a prophet to nations." **What is your name**? Like most of us, Jeremiah identified himself by his weaknesses and deficiencies and how he had been conditioned to see himself. But that does not deter God.

In His love for us, He continues to pursue us to believe in who He has made us to be, not the conditions or circumstances we were born into or grew up in. God's response to Jeremiah (and to us today) is stated in **verses 7-10**: "But the Lord said to me, 'Do not say, I am (only) a young man. Because everywhere I send you, you shall go. And whatever I command you, you shall speak. Do not be afraid of them (or their hostile faces), for I am with you (always), to protect you and deliver you.' Says the Lord."

"Then the Lord stretched out His Hand and touched my mouth, and the Lord said to me, 'Behold (hear Me), I have put My words in your mouth. See, I have appointed you this day over the nations and over the kingdoms, to uproot and break down, to destroy and to overthrow, to build and to plant.'"

When God shows us our identity, for most of us, it may take years of renewing our minds to be transformed into who God says we are. But the journey, the metamorphosis, is so worth it.

Do not ever give up on pursuing this. **What is your name**? This brings true self-confidence and assurance that humankind cannot take away from you. Let us go back to the demonically possessed man. **Luke 8: Verse 35** says, "And people came out to see what had happened. They came to Jesus and found the man from whom the demons had been cast out, sitting at Jesus' feet, clothed and in his right mind (mentally healthy)."

Emotional healing is available to everyone, though only a few people pursue it.

Verse 37 tells us that the people asked Jesus to leave their region or village because he drove the demons into a herd of pigs, who went over a cliff (which was their money, their bank, their hustle). Some want this world's riches rather than their souls' prosperity. Jesus taught us in **Mark 8: 36**, "For what does it profit or benefit a man to gain the whole world (with all its pleasures) and lose or forfeit his soul?"

Reflection:

Being in the ministry of spreading this good news should come after or while we are actively healing emotionally, which can only enhance our spiritual growth. **Verse 38** of **Luke 8** tells us, "But the man from whom the demons had gone out kept begging Him (Jesus), pleading to go with Him; but Jesus sent him away, saying, **Verse 39**, 'Return home and tell of all the great things God has done for you.'"

We are most effective in sharing the Good News of what God has done for and in us, in the area where we have been healed. We can talk the talk because we have walked the walk.

We speak and testify from personal experiences. I know how God has delivered me in many areas, especially emotionally. Understanding, embracing, and abiding in His unconditional love has transformed and continues to transform my life in ways that words cannot describe. And He wants to do the same for you.

We can only love ourselves and others to the degree we have been emotionally healed.

Prayer:

Most loving Father, I come to You, trusting in the finished work of my redemption and salvation by Your Son and my Savior, Jesus Christ. You are healing me deep within so I can live abundantly, free from the fear that once shackled me to my insecurities. As I am healed, use my life to tell others the Good News that You want also to love and heal them. Use my life for Your purpose and Your glory.

In Jesus' Name. Amen.

Day 5

Love That Forgives

Scripture: **Psalm 103:12**: "As far as the east is from the west, so far has He removed our transgressions from us."

Devotional:

One of the most beautiful aspects of God's unconditional love is His ability to forgive and restore us. Because of God's love, we can find redemption and forgiveness for our wrongdoings. This forgiveness is an expression of God's boundless compassion and mercy. Forgiveness relates to the action of repentance. Repentance involves acknowledging one's mistakes, expressing sincere remorse, and genuinely trying to change while cooperating with God's help. It is a necessary component in restoration, which we shall discuss later.

Forgiveness of our sins reconciles us to God Himself, bringing spiritual healing and renewal to our souls and restoring our relationship with God.

No matter how far we have strayed or how many times we have fallen, His love covers our sins (us missing the mark) and offers us a fresh start. As we continue to read **verses 13-14**, we are reminded that God loves us unconditionally and knows our fragility. Whenever I read **verse 12**, I always asked deep within me, how could He? Why would God so abundantly love someone like me? He knows me to my core. I could not believe that God would love me with all my faults and failings because I saw myself as unlovable. I measured His love by my conditions, through my "unworthy" eyes. But I have learned and honestly believe that God never loves us based on how we see ourselves. He loves us based on His character and who He has created us to be. **Verses 13 and 14** show us this love that we also feel for our children.

They state, "Just as a father (mother) loves his (her) children, so the Lord loves those who fear and worship Him (with awe-filled respect and deepest reverence). For He knows our (mortal) frame; He remembers that we are (merely) dust." God knows that we will struggle, fall, fail, and may even abandon Him; but again, His love is based on who He is, not on who we are.

I will say this repeatedly. Love was never a human concept. God invites us to get intimately acquainted with this love, with who He is. If you believe and hold on to this truth, it will set your soul free. It can begin a beautiful journey for you that will not only transform who you are into who you are meant to be, but will develop an unshakable faith, a hope beyond human comprehension. This love has the power to affect all those around you positively. **Verse 17** says, "But the lovingkindness of the Lord is from everlasting to everlasting on those who (reverently) fear Him, and His righteousness to (their) children's children."

Another aspect of God's forgiveness towards us is that it releases us from guilt and shame, two major components that hinder us from developing, growing, and transforming into His unique creations, full of potential and purpose. Believing in God's forgiveness can lift the burden of guilt, allowing us to find inner peace and move toward self-acceptance. Since we, with all our faults and failings, have been forgiven and loved so undeservingly, should we not forgive and extend love and grace to those struggling and hurting like we once were? **Colossians 3:13** states, "Bearing graciously with one another, and willingly forgiving each other, if one has a cause for complaint against another; just as the Lord has forgiven you, so should you forgive." Forgiveness has nothing to do with whether you are right or wrong. You may be in your right to be hurt and offended. Still, forgiveness is also for you, for your heart to be untainted, undamaged, healed, and free, even if the offender never apologizes.

Unforgiveness blocks your access to divine unconditional love because love and hate cannot coexist. It is your choice. Hold onto hate and become bitter, or release forgiveness and be free to continue receiving divine love to flow in and through you. I have been in both places, and believe me, love is a better spiritual and emotional state in which to live. Forgiveness is not easily done. However, if you can process that hurt people, hurt people, and that they are in an emotionally tortured place within themselves, as so many of us are or were, it can move us to release not only the perpetrator but ourselves from a self-imposed prison sentence.

Romans 5:8 states, "But God clearly shows and proves His own love for us, by the fact that while we were still sinners, Christ died for us." Forgiveness is not about justice. Forgiveness is about love, an expression of God's love, an act of compassion, and a way to cultivate healthy relationships and promote healing in our immediate and extended communities.

Forgiveness plays a crucial role in our personal growth and spiritual development. **1 Peter 4:8** says, "Above all, have fervent and unfailing love for one another, because love covers a multitude of sins (it overlooks unkindness and unselfishly seeks the best for others)." God, in His marvelous love for us, sent His Son, Jesus Christ, to cover our sins and pay the death penalty for us. When we begin to meditate on the price of the cross that Jesus bore for us, we can start to get some insight into the power, the redemptive power, of His marvelous love. Accepting this truth and forgiveness frees us spiritually in so many ways.

John 3:16 is a famous and one of the most recognized and memorized scriptures. It says, "For God so (greatly) loved and dearly prized the world, that He (even)gave His (one and) only begotten Son, so that whoever believes and trusts in Him (as Savior) shall not perish, but have eternal life." God loves us and allows us to choose His love and forgiveness.

The penalty for our sins has already been paid. If we believe and accept God's offer of forgiveness, we have eternal life with Him when we leave this earth. Not only do we have forgiveness, but we are also restored to fellowship with Him in the Edenic state. It is that simple. This is one of the compelling benefits of forgiveness. It redemptively restores. It brings us back to our former state and Edenic condition, place, and position. It repairs and reinstates what was broken in us.

As a medical professional, I have researched the many physical benefits attributed to forgiveness. Forgiveness reduces stress levels, lowers blood pressure, strengthens the immune system, improves heart health, and decreases symptoms of depression and anxiety, to name a few (I will note here that it is a complex and personal process that varies from individual to individual).

Ephesians 4:32, "Be kind to one another, tenderhearted, forgiving one another, as God in Christ forgave you."

One of the extraordinary aspects of God's unconditional love is His ability to forgive us. God's forgiveness is limitless and extends to every aspect of our lives. Similarly, we are called to forgive others as we have been forgiven. I know for many, this is easier said than done. When I have been deeply hurt, my former mindset was God, only You can forgive to this depth. I felt incapable of forgiving deeply malicious atrocities done to myself, loved ones, or defenseless people until I understood that I loved conditionally, which made me lack the capacity to be empathetic and understanding. So, how many times do I forgive someone (particularly for the same offense)? The answer is as many opportunities as possible to learn how to love them unconditionally. Again, this is not a human concept. It is a supernatural power given to us by God.

Luke 7:47 says, he who forgives little, loves little; he who forgives much, loves much (paraphrased).

Look at opportunities to forgive as opportunities to learn how to love unconditionally. I also believe that God is a just God, and because of His love for me and others, He is and always will be a defender of the defenseless. I may not see His justice or grace meted out, but I know He is my Defender. **Psalms 62:6** teaches us, "He ONLY is my rock and my salvation, My fortress, and my DEFENSE; I will not be shaken or discouraged." This topic of forgiveness needs a book by itself. Still, I have come to understand, believe, and embrace the truth that you cannot love unconditionally without being able and willing to forgive.

Reflection:

Today, let us reflect on the depth of God's forgiveness. May we find solace in His grace and extend that same forgiveness to ourselves and others. Take a moment to reflect on a time when you experienced the forgiveness of God's love. How did it change your perspective and approach to life?

Consider any areas where you may struggle to forgive yourself or others, and ask God to help you release those burdens. Allow the love of God to bring healing to those areas. Take a moment to contemplate the power of forgiveness in your life. How has God's forgiveness impacted you? Consider any grudges, anger, or bitterness you may be holding onto and invite God into those areas to heal and restore to you a forgiving heart. Pray for strength and humility to extend forgiveness to others, just as God forgave you.

Personal Experience: As I continue my journey in learning how to love others the way God loves me, I made a **decision** (for to love is a decision) to forgive my siblings for what I held in my heart, for the hurts they have caused me (this is subjective). I chose to forgive them before I ventured on vacation back to my homeland of Trinidad and Tobago to celebrate my son's birthday and pay tribute to my mom's only living sibling, the matriarch of our family, my aunt Veronica.

I had held my elder brother at an emotional distance for many years (loving him from afar, I would say) but did not realize it was only my self-imposed defense mechanism against being hurt.

My brother is a hugger and kisser (as all the family knows), and he showered me with hugs and kisses that I finally embraced. I weep now as I recollect that precious moment.

This was a healing experience for him, me, and all my family members who knew our history. God showed me that true forgiveness can only be a by-product of unconditionally loving others. Forgiving and letting go of hurts become easier when we love others as He loves us. In the forgiving comes the healing of wounds, emotions, and relationships. This is a tangible and practical example of what I have been learning along this journey. And He is not done with me yet.

Here are some ways forgiveness can contribute to these areas of your life, in addition to spiritual healing:

1. Emotional Healing: When we hold on to anger, resentment, or bitterness, it can weigh us down emotionally and hinder our personal growth. Forgiveness allows us to release these negative emotions and create space for healing. By choosing to forgive, we free ourselves from emotional burdens, experience inner peace, and open the door to personal growth.

2. Self-Reflection and Growth: Forgiving others requires self-reflection, empathy, and understanding. It encourages us to see situations from different perspectives and challenges us to grow in compassion and sensitivity. Through forgiveness, we develop self-awareness, learn from our experiences, and evolve as individuals.

3. Strengthening Relationships: Forgiveness can repair and enhance relationships. When we forgive others, we create opportunities for reconciliation and rebuilding trust.

Forgiveness fosters empathy, communication, and a willingness to understand one another. By practicing forgiveness, we contribute to healthier and more fulfilling relationships, which are essential for personal growth and spiritual well-being.

4. Cultivating Compassion and Love: Forgiveness is an act of compassion and love. By forgiving others, we cultivate these qualities within ourselves. It helps us develop greater empathy, understanding, and acceptance of the imperfections in ourselves and others. Cultivating compassion and love contributes to personal growth and deepens our spiritual connection with God and others (**Matthew 22:37-40**). Forgiveness deepens our spiritual connection, bringing us closer to our faith, inner peace, and a sense of purpose.

It is a personal journey, and the process may differ for everyone. It requires time, patience, and self-reflection.

Prayer:

Gracious Father, thank You for the forgiveness and restoration You offer through Your unconditional love. Help us to embrace Your forgiveness and extend it to others fully. Help us embody the spirit of forgiveness in our relationships so that we may emulate Your love.

Heal any wounds or hurts in our lives, and grant us the grace to forgive others as you have forgiven us. Give us the strength to release bitterness or resentment, and fill us with Your love and compassion. Heavenly Father, thank You for Your forgiveness, which knows no bounds.

In Jesus' Name, Amen

Reflection/Note-taking

_____

_____

_____

_____

_____

_____

Reflection/Note-taking

_____

_____

_____

_____

_____

Day 6

A Love That Restores

Scripture: **Psalm 23:3**: "He refreshes and restores my soul (a person's moral or emotional nature or sense of identity); He leads me in paths of righteousness for His name's sake."

Devotional:

God's unconditional love is not only forgiving and sacrificial, but it also has the power to restore. Forgiveness opens the door to restoration, defined as returning something (or someone) to a former owner, place, or its original condition. No matter how broken or weary we may feel, God's love can heal and restore our souls. As He restores us, we can restore the fractured relationships in our lives if the other parties are willing. Today, let us meditate on the healing power of God's love and seek His restoration in our lives. So, what does He restore us to? I will reiterate here that we are made in His image and likeness.

Yes, by the power of His Holy Spirit, we too can have the characteristics of God (**1 John 4:17**). I know that is difficult to imagine since we have lived in a conditionally sinful state for so long, but this is God's heart and desire for us. He wants to bring us back to an Edenic relationship with Him and has opened that path with the sacrifice of His Son, Jesus Christ. Christ paid the penalty for sin's separation so that we now have free access to this beautiful, dynamic relationship with God that transforms and restores us. If you are like me, you sometimes get weary physically, mentally, emotionally, and yes, spiritually. Sometimes, loving the unlovely aspects of people drains everything out of me. That is my cue to step aside and take some time to refill my emotional, spiritual, and physical batteries, plug into the Source of life, and get recharged. That may be some quiet time with scriptural meditation. I have the perfect spot on my back patio where I read scriptures and inspirational or emotionally healing books and meditate upon the application of their meaning to my life.

I also love listening to music from different genres, but especially worship music to which I sing or dance. I enjoy walking and going to the gym, but walking in the cool of the day and admiring nature around me helps to bring me back to my center of serenity. Another hobby I have is cooking, creating healthy, tasty recipes that can complement my low-carb, high-protein dietary lifestyle. Think of some things you can incorporate in your daily life for self-care, incorporating all the areas I have discussed. An aspect of God restoring our souls is cooperating with Him in caring for the entirety of our being, spiritual, emotional, and physical. When we neglect one area, it affects the other areas as well.

Reflection:

Reflect on moments when you experienced God's restoring love. How did it impact you and renew your spirit? Consider any areas needing restoration and invite God into those spaces. Pray for the strength and perseverance to follow His leading as He restores and transforms you.

Personal Experience: While on vacation in Trinidad (see Day 5), I sat on my niece's patio, studying and meditating on the scriptures, especially **Psalm 23:3**, "He refreshes and restores my soul (my life); He leads me in paths of righteousness for His name's sake." I thought of the non-existent relationship with my estranged sister, the only living sister I had left on this earth. I thought of what God had been teaching and healing within me regarding loving others unconditionally. His command to love others as he loves us brought the realization that I had never known how to love my sister (or anyone else) this way. Both of our actions and reactions had affected our tumultuous relationship over the years. But at this point, none of that mattered to me. What was important was my reactions to her, which were based on all the "conditions" I required for her to be a recipient of my love. As you may know, conditional love is not love but a self-serving transaction. Unconditional love is not selfish, self-seeking, or self-centered (**1 Corinthians 13:5**).

Love only thinks of the best interests of others without wanting anything back in return. So I knew what I needed to do. According to **Psalm 103:12**, I chose to cast all her wrongdoings (mine as well) into that sea of forgetfulness, removing them as far as the east is from the west, to remember them no more. **Psalms 103: 15-16** (paraphrased) reminded me that our human life is like grass; it blooms like a wildflower, but when the wind blows through it, it is gone. Even the ground where we stand does not remember it. I have two siblings who are no longer here on this earth with me, but God has left me with two more that I can learn how to love.

I had reached out to my sister through her son to connect with her while I was in my homeland. She initially said no, and I was ok with that because I knew my decision to love her was not based on her response. In learning how to love unconditionally, I also understood that this type of love had more to do with the giver than the receiver.

I accepted and respected her decision and thought that was the end of it. A few days later, I received a call from my elder son, Jonathan, asking me to contact my sister. I told him she was not ready and I would respect that. He said, "Mom, you literally have your two sons and nephew praying right now for reconciliation between you and Aunty Donna, and she reached out to say she wanted to see you. Mom, please reach out to her. Mom, this is God moving."

I do not have to tell you the emotions that ran through me as I became aware of how much this meant to others besides me, and I also believed God was moving in ways I could never have. I obeyed, reached out, and met with my sister. That day, **Psalms 23:3** was realized in the flesh as God restored our souls and led us down paths for His Name's sake. Unconditional love not only forgives but also restores. God's forgiveness is often understood as a means of healing and restoring the relationship between God and the individual.

It is seen as an opportunity for spiritual growth and transformation. It allows individuals to move forward from past mistakes and experience reconciliation with their faith in God and others. This restoration involves healing the wounds, hurts, and traumas we may have experienced, bringing wholeness and inner peace to our souls.

Continue with this devotional, exploring different aspects of God's unconditional love each day and providing space for reflection, prayer, and growth in understanding and experiencing this incredible love. Allow God's love to shape and transform your life, and may you become a vessel of His love to those around you. Restoration happens when wounds are healed, minds are transformed, spirits find rest, and life changes, all for our good, **Jeremiah 29:11**. God's love can bring healing and restore our souls. In **John 10: 10**, Jesus tells us that He came that we may have life and have it in abundance (to the full, till it overflows). This is what we have free access to.

The Bible teaches that God is our shepherd, leading and guiding us in the paths of righteousness. God provides wisdom, discernment, and guidance through His Holy Spirit to restore our souls. He leads us away from destructive paths and towards righteous living, enabling us to find purpose and fulfillment. God invites us to find rest and renewal in His presence.

Psalm 23:2-3 says, "He leads me beside still waters; He restores my soul." This imagery suggests that God offers refreshment and nourishment to our weary souls. Through prayer, worship, and meditation on His Word, we can experience spiritual refreshment and renewal. We also benefit from deliverance, sustenance, and God's provision through restoration. God is also a Deliverer, rescuing us from captivity and bondage (unforgiveness being one of them). He has the power to free us from the chains of sin, guilt, and shame, restoring our souls to a state of freedom.

Debra Enile Armand

Through the work of Jesus Christ, we can experience liberation and a renewed sense of purpose and joy. God promises to provide for our every need. In restoring our souls, He meets our physical, emotional, and spiritual needs. Just as a shepherd cares for His flock, God supplies us with sustenance, comfort, and nourishment, fulfilling the deepest longings of our souls.

<u>Prayer:</u>

Loving Father, thank you for your restorative love. Heal and restore us,

body, mind, and soul. Lead us in paths of righteousness and show us how to live according to your will. Pour out your love upon us and renew our spirits. May we live as testimonies of your restoring love to the world.

In Jesus' Name, Amen.

Reflection/Note-taking

_____

_____

_____

_____

_____

Debra Enile Armand

Reflection/Note-taking

_____

_____

_____

_____

_____

Day 7

Love That Gives Freely

Scripture: **John 3:16**: "For God so loved the world that He gave His one and only Son, that whoever believes in Him shall not perish but have eternal life."

Devotional:

Love is about freedom, freedom to choose, freedom to receive, freedom to give. Love that is offered freely is a hallmark of God's unconditional love for us. He did not withhold His most precious gift, Jesus Christ, but offered Him as a sacrifice for our sins. **Romans 8:32** says, "He (God), who did not spare (even) His own Son, but gave Him up for us all, how will He not also, along with Him, graciously give us all things?" Jesus had the power and ability to withhold His life and not die on the cross for us, but He chose to freely lay down His life as a ransom for us to have access to the Father. In **John 10:18**, Jesus says, "No one takes it (His Life) away from Me, but I lay it down voluntarily.

I am authorized and have power to lay it down and to give it up, and I am authorized and have power to take it back. This command I received from My Father."

What can we learn about the freedom in this type of love? Knowing that God loves me because He chooses to is liberating. I love a song called "Jireh" by Elevation Worship, and part of it says, "I am already loved, I am already chosen. I know who I am. I know what You have spoken. I am already loved, more than I can imagine, and that is enough." Those words have been my anthem for the last few years of living and believing in God's love for me. My everyday life now focuses on loving others and giving them the freedom to make their own choices (which they will anyway).

As a single woman, this has a profound importance in my life because I no longer wait for someone to choose me. I am already chosen. I no longer wait for someone to love me. I am already loved more than I could imagine.

It is liberating to know that choosing a future mate will be based on other important factors, not on how they can make me "feel" about myself. I know who I am because of what God has spoken about me. That is freedom. It is exhilaratingly emancipating to know that I can be at peace and still love individuals who make their own choices based on what is in their best interests (even if that does not include me).

Allowing others to be their authentic self in your presence, being who you are, and feeling safe to do so is freedom. When the validity of our existence and worth is not based on other people's opinions of who we are, their choices will not cause us to feel rejected because we know we are already chosen. Loving others with their best interests at heart and not wanting anything in return (selflessly) does not come easily or naturally. It comes from God poured into you, and God poured out of you, into others, and it may take daily reminders before you are living, breathing, and walking in this Truth. Love is about freedom.

Because of this freedom, we can freely give. We can give of ourselves, our time, our resources. It is a natural by-product of love.

2 Corinthians 9:7 says, "Let each one give (thoughtfully and with purpose) just as he has decided in his heart, not grudgingly or under compulsion, for God loves a cheerful giver (and delights in the one whose heart is in his gift." Cheerful giving can be applied to other areas besides monetary contributions. Giving from a heart of pure love is the most peaceful and rewarding thing you can do because you are not looking for anything in return, including acknowledgment, accolades, applauses, likes or follows on social media, etc.

Today, let us meditate on selfless giving at the core of God's love (**John 3:16**). May we learn from His example and seek opportunities to love and give to others sacrificially.

Reflection:

Reflect on how God's love manifests in your life through His selfless giving. Consider the gifts and blessings you have received and how they have shaped you. As I think about this, it reminds me of the burning passion within to give this gift of God's Good News to others so they, too, can be set free of an unrewarding life of conditional love. This is part of my calling: giving back and using my life experiences and wisdom gained along the way to help others. We are not containers of God's love as it is poured into us to be kept within us. We are conduits with a spout that pours out as His love is poured in. The more we pour out to others, the more capacity we have to receive more and more of His marvelous love.

Take a moment to think of ways you can imitate this giving in your relationships and community. Ask God to show you opportunities to extend His love through acts of kindness and generosity.

Continue with this devotional, exploring different aspects of God's unconditional love each day and providing space for reflection, prayer, and growth in understanding and experiencing this incredible love demonstrated through giving.

<u>Prayer</u>:

Heavenly Father, thank you for the immeasurable gift of your Son, Jesus Christ.

Help us to understand the power of selfless giving and enable us to love and give freely as you have loved and given to us. Open our eyes to the needs of others and guide us in acts of kindness and generosity.

In Jesus' Name, Amen.

Day 8

Love That Never Fails

Scripture: **1 Corinthians 13:8a**: "Love never fails."

Devotional:

The love of God is unwavering and unending. It is a love that never fails, no matter the circumstances or failures we may face. God's love never fails because He is Faithful and has called us to love ourselves and others the way He loves us. God's Love is "Emet." The biblical meaning of this word used to describe the character of God is Faithfulness and Truth. When it says God is "full of Emet," it means He is trustworthy. Until I truly learned and embraced God's unconditional love for me, I had difficulty trusting Him when I endured adverse circumstances. I would question His love for me. Through this journey, I have His love for me solidified in my heart, mind, and spirit. His love never fails because He is Emet, faithful, and trustworthy.

There have been people and things I have placed my trust in that have failed me because they were not emet. I know I have failed others similarly since I was not full of emet. Some may question if we can love this way. And I say to you, yes, yes, and yes. But you can only do so through God's power and grace through His Spirit living within you. This love is spiritual because, again, it only comes from God. It is God, and God is a Spirit. God was before the beginning, and He will be past the end. He is infinite and eternal. Thus, the reason this love will never fail. It will never end. It will be with us throughout our lifetime and beyond when we transition from this earth. This love will not fail us during tragic times or sufferings. It will not fail you in your darkest moments.

This love transcends every boundary and is freely given to all, regardless of our flaws and shortcomings. It reminds me of the woman caught in adultery (**John 8:1-11**): Jesus shows compassion and forgiveness to this woman.

Rather than condemning her, He offers forgiveness and encourages her to change her ways. This example highlights God's mercy and grace, emphasizing His love that never fails. No matter your circumstances, it will not fail. Even when we are faithless, He remains faithful.

In Hebrew, the word for truth, emet, contains the first, middle, and last letters of the Hebrew alphabet, indicating that truth encompasses all things and endures from beginning to end (hebrews4christians.com). Not only is emet Faithfulness, but it is also Truth. God is Truth. We should learn to walk and live in truth. By being a truthful person, you become a trustworthy person, a faithful person, and a person full of emet, and that never fails. God's love never fails, and He is faithful and trustworthy. He is Truth. Today, let us meditate on the steadfastness of God's love and find comfort and security in knowing that His love for us will always endure.

May we exhibit this same unwavering love in our relationships, knowing that love that never fails can transform lives.

Reflection:

Reflect on moments when you experienced God's faithfulness and His trustworthiness. How did it impact you and help you navigate challenging times? Consider any areas in your relationships where you may struggle to exhibit this love. Ask God for His guidance and strength to love without fail. Embrace the truth that His love is always available to you, regardless of your circumstances.

Prayer:

Loving Father, thank you for your steadfast and unwavering love. Help us trust in Your love that never fails and exhibit the same love in our relationships.

Teach us to love others unconditionally, just as you have loved us. Fill us with your Holy Spirit so we may be vessels of Your unfailing love.

In Jesus' Name, Amen.

Day 9

Love That Gives Hope

Scripture: **Romans 15:13**: "May the God of hope fill you with all joy and peace as you trust in him, so that you may overflow with hope by the power of the Holy Spirit."

Devotional:

It is very fitting to follow the previous devotion on love that never fails. When we believe that God is full of emet and can help transform us into His image and likeness, this gives us hope. It allows us to switch our dependence on human love and expectations. As God's Spirit dwells in us and pours His love in and through us, we can still love those who have failed us or whom we have failed. This gives us hope. **Romans 5:5** says, "Such hope (in God's Promises) NEVER disappoints us, because God's love has been abundantly poured out within our hearts through the Holy Spirit Who was given to us."

The hope we attain from God's love is mighty.

Listen to what **Isaiah 40:31** says: "But those who wait for the Lord (who expect, look for, and hope in Him) will gain new strength and renew their power; they will lift their wings (and rise close to God) like eagles (rising toward the sun); They will run and not become weary, they will walk and not grow tired."

I know we all have lost hope during difficult seasons in our lives. I know I have. When I lost my mom at the tender age of 20 (she was 45 years old), my world crumbled because I felt, up to that time, she was the only earthly person who loved me and looked out for my best interest. She became my world. When she had a sudden cardiac arrest and died, a part of me died. In fact, I wanted to die, and I tried to take my own life. **Proverbs 13: 12** says, "Hope deferred makes the heart sick."

Delayed hope crushes the heart. Hope deferred, delayed, put off, or prolonged can lead to anxiety, depression, or even physical sicknesses.

I am not a therapist; I only speak from my personal experiences and of those whom I have known who have gone through similar circumstances.

But God's emet (Faithfulness) was there with me at the lowest point in my life. A compassionate nurse on the unit took me to her home upon my discharge and spiritually and emotionally nursed me back to a place of stability. She shared how much God loved me and that I was not alone. That gave me hope. The unconditional love of God fills our hearts with hope. It is a love that brings joy and peace, even during difficult circumstances. Today, let us focus on the hope that comes from knowing and experiencing God's love. May we find encouragement and strength in His promises, and may His love motivate us to share this hope with others.

Reflection:

Reflect on moments when you felt the powerful hope from God's love.

How did it impact your outlook on life and your ability to persevere? Consider any areas where you may feel hopeless and ask God to renew your faith and fill you with His hope. Pray for opportunities to share this hope with those around you who may be in need.

Prayer:

Heavenly Father, thank you for the hope found in your unconditional love. Fill us with joy and peace as we trust in you, and empower us to overflow with hope through the power of your Holy Spirit. Renew our faith in times of despair, and grant us the courage to share this hope with others.

In Jesus' Name, Amen.

Day 10

Love That Calls Us to Love

Scripture: **1 John 4:11:** "Dear friends, since God so loved us, we also ought to love one another."

<u>Devotional</u>:

The unconditional love of God calls us to love one another. As recipients of His love, we are called to extend that love to those around us. This has been and continues to be a practicing journey for me. Because of my learned conditional love and unhealed emotional wounds, I could only love others to the capacity of my healing, emotional intelligence, and the love I felt for myself, which was two on a scale of ten. In this magnificent journey of **Matthew 22:37-40**, I continue to believe how much I am loved, know my identity in Christ, and now love others from the love daily poured into me by Christ.

Our scripture verse of **1 John 4:11** begins with "Since God so loved us." Love never originated in the human mind.

It is not a human concept, so we must learn of love from its source, God. **1 John 4:19** says, "We love, because He (God) first loved us." Ephesians 2:4 says, "God, being (so very) rich in mercy, because of His great and wonderful love with which He loved us." **1 John 4:10** reminds us, "In this is love, not that we loved God, but that He loved us and sent His Son to be the propitiation (that is, the atoning sacrifice and satisfying offering) for our sins (fulfilling God's requirement for justice against sin and placating His wrath)." And how can I not mention one of the most quoted scriptures you probably know, **John 3:16**, "For God so Loved the world, that He gave His only begotten Son, that whosoever believes in Him, shall not perish but have everlasting life."

God initiated, paid for, and now sustains a love relationship and pursuit with each person on the face of the earth. We do not seek Him. He came after us.

I am learning that the more I abide, stay connected, and seek after His love, He fills me to overflowing. It is a daily pursuit for me.

It is not a one-and-done. The more He loves me, the more I love Him. The more I love Him, the more I can love others. I know that I have done nothing to deserve this unconditional love. A dear friend asked, "He can love even a wretch like me?" And my answer was yes, even more so. Because I, too, am that wretch that He loved the same when I was "tore up from the floor up" as He loves the transforming me today. It is a love so undeserved but freely given. How can I not give this love to others as He continues to heal me from the inside out? I sometimes feel like Peter when he said in Acts 3:6, "Silver and gold I do not have: but what I do have I give to you." For me, this is loving others as God loves me. This incredible journey is filled with continuous learning of God's love. I may fail at times, but what a fulfilling experience. This love, God's love, cannot be contained within my human flesh.

I must pour it out on others. Today, let us reflect on the call to love others as God loves us.

May we seek opportunities to demonstrate this love and be intentional in our relationships, always looking for ways to show kindness, compassion, and forgiveness.

Reflection:

Reflect on the ways you can actively love and serve others in your daily life. Consider any areas where you may struggle to love unconditionally and ask God for guidance and transformation. Pray for a heart willing and open to love others, no matter the circumstances.

Continue with this devotional, exploring different aspects of God's unconditional love each day and providing space for reflection, prayer, and growth in understanding and experiencing this incredible love. Allow God's love to shape and transform your life, and may you become a vessel of His love to those around you.

Prayer:

Gracious God, thank you for calling us to love one another, not with our understanding of love, which is often conditional. Help us to love as You have loved us, with kindness, compassion, and forgiveness. Open our eyes to the needs of those around us and give us the courage to act in love. May our lives be a testament to Your unconditional love.

In Jesus' Name, Amen.

Day 11

Love That Sacrifices

Scripture: <u>John 15:13</u>: "Greater love has no one than this: to lay down one's life for one's friends."

<u>Devotional:</u>

The epitome of love is sacrifice. Jesus demonstrated the depth of God's love by willingly laying down His life for us. This sacrificial love is a powerful reminder of the lengths God will go to for our redemption and restoration. After celebrating my son's 33rd birthday in my homeland of Trinidad and Tobago, my childhood friend, Bianca Beckles-Sargent, said something to me that caused me to think more deeply about this aspect of unconditional love. She mentioned that she had such a great time at the party. She said she knew this was costly (monetarily), but sometimes uniting family/people together costs.

I acknowledged the material sacrifice of getting family from two sides of the world together, some, like my son, who had not seen my side of the family for 20 years. Some families had not spoken to each other in years. It did cost to bring all of them together, but the sacrifice was worth every joyous tear we shed as we hugged, embraced, and kissed each other in love. Friends felt like family, and family became friends. The love that night was so tangible that we still remember it today. Loving someone may cost us our pride (to apologize and reconcile), cost us choosing to release grudges, infractions, unhealed emotional wounds and give hugs instead (this happened between my elder brother and I), so we forgive, we are restored, and we are healed. You see, unconditional love, God's love, heals.

Loving us cost God in giving up His only begotten Son. Loving us cost Jesus in willingly sacrificing His life on the cross to be eternally united to all who would believe and receive His love.

Sometimes, to love like God will be sacrificial, but look at the fantastic benefits beyond the Cross, beyond the emotional wounds, the division, the hurt, and anger. God's love heals. It heals our relationship first with our heavenly Father and can heal and restore our earthly relationships. It did for me, on what I thought was a surprise birthday party for my beloved son. The earthly sacrifices cannot compare to the heavenly and spiritual miracles that my family and I received on this eventful vacation.

So yes, loving others, especially those closest to us may cost us many things – forgiving them seventy times seven in one day- but what we receive in return far outweighs what we lay down at the foot of the same cross where Jesus laid down His life.

In return, we are resurrected from death within us (our relationship with God and ourselves) and death outside our earthly relationships. Today, let us reflect on the sacrificial love of Jesus and how it transforms our lives.

May we be inspired to love sacrificially and serve others with selflessness and humility. What can you sacrifice today for the sake of love?

<u>Reflection</u>:

Reflect on Jesus' sacrificial love and its impact on your life. How does His example challenge you to love others sacrificially? Consider any areas you may be holding back from or struggling to serve and sacrifice for others. Pray for the Holy Spirit to strengthen you and allow you to love selflessly.

<u>Prayer</u>:

Gracious God, thank you for Jesus's sacrificial love. Teach us to lay down our lives for others, just as He laid down His life for us. Please help us serve selflessly and put the needs of others before our own. Fill us with your love and compassion so that we may reflect your sacrificial love to those around us.

In Jesus' Name, Amen.

Debra Enile Armand

Day 12

Love That Empowers

Scripture: **2 Timothy 1:7**: "For God has not given us a spirit of fear, but of power and of love and of a sound mind."

Devotional:

God's love empowers us to live boldly and confidently in Him. It drives out fear. **1 John 4:18** states, "There is no fear in love (dread does not exist) because perfect (complete, full-grown, mature) love drives out fear, because fear involves punishment, so the one who is afraid is not perfected in love (has not grown into a sufficient understanding of God's love)." God's love gives us the strength to overcome any obstacle or challenge that comes our way.

We can look at empowerment in many ways to affect our lives in a direction of divine purpose.

I think of empowerment as the ability to change from the inside out.

For many years, I felt helpless in my emotional healing and, at times, prayed and left everything up to God to miraculously make all the pain disappear. I have cried many tears and prayed many prayers but did not know how to heal the hurts within. Sometimes, I became disappointed with God and turned away from Him because I was not seeing or getting the results I wanted. This scripture has a different meaning for me now in this love journey. James 2:26 says, "For just as the (human) body without the Spirit is dead (seriously think about that), so faith without works is also dead." I am not talking about trying to work for our salvation or to be accepted by God. That work is finished on the cross by Jesus' sacrifice and freely given to all who will believe and receive it.

The works I am referring to are the actions we must take in cooperating with God, through the help of His Holy Spirit, towards our inner healing.

The Holy Spirit is the only One who can empower us to forgive the unforgivable as His love flows in and through us. The Holy Spirit will empower us daily to overcome seemingly insurmountable challenges and propel us into our divine destiny. At times, it may be visible manifestations and, at other times, subtle inward changes that set us free from the chains of our past experiences.

We have a part to play in our healing. For example, if we are overweight and desperately want to live a healthier lifestyle, sitting on the sofa and eating cookies and ice cream will not bring us the results we desire, no matter how long or hard we pray. Trust me, I have been there and said my blessings over many unhealthy foods, asking God to let them nourish my body. I still gained over 49 pounds over the years, with accompanying food-related diseases.

When I began the journey to Soul Freedom (my first book), my eating habits changed. I got off the sofa and began to walk, then went to the gym and lost those 49 unhealthy, prayer-filled pounds.

God will give us the power we need to live an abundant life. **2 Peter 1:3** (NIV) says, "His divine power has given us everything we need for a godly life through our knowledge of Him, who has called us by His glory and goodness." Today, let us reflect on the empowering love of God and how it enables us to live a life of purpose and courage. Knowing His Holy Spirit has equipped us, we lean on His power and love to navigate life.

Reflection:

Think about moments when you have felt empowered by God's love. How did it enable you to face challenges and step out in faith? Consider any areas where fear may hinder you and pray for God to replace it with His empowering love.

<u>Prayer</u>:

Most loving Father, teach me and show me by living examples how I can submit myself to the empowerment of Your Holy Spirit living in me. All I know is how to rely on my willpower. I know and accept the responsibility for my part in this journey because You said that faith without actions is dead work. Teach me, Lord. My heart is open.

In Jesus' Name, Amen.

Day 13

Love That Encourages

Scripture: <u>1Thessalonians 5:11</u>: "Therefore encourage one another and build one another up, just as you are doing."

<u>Devotional</u>:

God's love not only encourages us, but it also calls us to be encouragers to one another. I intend to encourage not just one but many through these pages. Today, we live in a world filled with negativity. Reality shows, music, movies, and the media glorify human psychological traumas that sell and bring billions to its marketers. God has always and continues to extend His love to a world in desperate need. We all have a choice in the paths we take. In **Matthew 7:13-14**, Jesus taught His followers to "Enter through the narrow gate.

For wide is the gate and broad and easy to travel is the path that leads the way to destruction and eternal loss, and there are many who enter through it.

But small is the gate and narrow and difficult to travel, is the path that leads the way to (everlasting) life, and there are few who find it." I can identify with these scriptures because loving conditionally (selfishly, only seeking my interests) is easier.

This path of unlearning love and learning unconditional love is sometimes challenging because you are learning how to die to your selfish nature. The rewards, thus far, have outweighed the sacrifices. This love journey is the most profound and best endeavor I have ever embarked upon, not only for myself but for those I interact with daily. It is a continuous journey that will last my lifetime, but I will never return to the life I once lived. This goes far beyond an unlearning journey.

It is a profound spiritual, emotional, and physical experience to have God's unconditional love live inside of you and be poured out through you. It changes you for the better.

Today, let us reflect on the importance of encouragement and how we can be vessels of God's love in this way. Our words, actions, and presence can uplift and inspire those around us. May we seek opportunities to build others up, speaking life-giving words and offering support and encouragement.

Reflection:

Consider times when others have encouraged you with their words or actions. How did it impact you and lift your spirits? Reflect on how you can be a source of encouragement to those around you. Pray for discernment to recognize when someone needs encouragement and the wisdom to provide it.

Prayer:

Gracious God, thank You for the gift of encouragement. Show us how to be a source of strength and inspiration to those who need it. Help us see the needs of others and offer words of encouragement that bring life and hope. Fill our hearts with Your love so that it may overflow and bless those around us. In Jesus' Name, Amen.

91

Day 14

Love That Rejoices

Scripture: <u>Romans 12:15</u>: "Rejoice with those who rejoice, weep with those who weep."

<u>Devotional:</u>

God's love calls us to rejoice with those who rejoice and weep with those who weep. It invites us to enter the joys and sorrows of others, showing compassion and empathy. I recall **1 Corinthians 13**. I call it the love Chapter. **Verse 1 says**, "If I speak with the tongues of men and of angels, but have not love (a profound thoughtfulness and unselfish concern for others, regardless of their circumstances or station in life, growing out of God's love for me), then I have become only a noisy gong or a clanging cymbal (just an annoying distraction)." Love meets people where they are, not where we want them to be.

It can allow us to enter their experiences as they invite us to, without taking it personally or trying to "fix" their circumstances for them. Unconditional love celebrates others' victories (it is not jealous). Since this love has the best interest of others at heart, we can rejoice and be exuberantly happy for others.

Our verse today has another part to it. It says to weep with those who weep. Again, unconditional love can enter another's experiences and stay with them as long as needed. Love is patient. Every one of us goes through something at some time. In our days of weeping, it is good to know that someone is truly there for and with us and genuinely loves us. God is always with us spiritually, showing us humanly that He is with us as He sends His servants to walk us through our most trying times. In some of my darkest moments involving the death of my sister and younger brother, God sent people beside me as I walked through that grief.

Some talked, and some stayed silent by my side. Some checked on me periodically as they gave me the space I needed. Some wept with me as I wept.

Debra Enile Armand

One of the shortest verses in the Bible, found in **John 11:35**, says, "Jesus wept." This was at the death of His friend Lazarus. You can read the entire chapter where He eventually raised Lazarus from the dead, and people questioned why Jesus did not prevent Lazarus' death. For our scripture today, I want you to see that the Son of God, in human form, experienced the same emotions that we do today. Jesus entered Mary and Martha's grief (the sisters of Lazarus) and wept as they wept. As you read more about His relationship with these siblings, you will see He also had joyous times with them, and when tragedy struck, He did not shy away. Jesus was not aloof on the sidelines. He entered their experience and wept with them.

1 Corinthians 13:2, "And if I have the gift of prophecy (and speak a new message from God to the people), and understand all mysteries, and (possess) all knowledge; and if I have all (sufficient) faith so that I can remove mountains, but do not have love (reaching out to others), I am nothing."

94

Today, let us reflect on the importance of rejoicing with others and lifting them in their moments of joy. May we celebrate alongside them, sharing in their happiness and express gratitude for the blessings in their lives. May we enter the invited spaces of those going through tumultuous and dark times and ask God for discerning words of life to encourage them. We can stay silent and weep with them as we love them through their pain.

Reflection:

Think about times when you have experienced the joy of others. How did it affect you and deepen your relationships? Reflect on any areas where you may struggle to rejoice with others genuinely. Pray for a heart of compassion and a spirit of gratitude so that you may genuinely celebrate and support others in their joys. Think of a time when you wept with someone completely heartbroken and crushed. Or you missed an opportunity to show them love by avoiding an "uncomfortable" experience. Ask God to love others unconditionally through you.

Debra Enile Armand

Prayer:

Heavenly Father, thank You for the gift of joy, empathy, and compassion. Help us to rejoice with others and celebrate their blessings. Please give us the empathy to weep with those who weep and to enter their sorrows with compassion.

Fill our hearts with love and gratitude so that we may be sources of encouragement and support.

In Jesus' Name, Amen.

Day 15

Love That Endures

Scripture: **1 Corinthians 13:7 (ESV)**: "Love bears all things, believes all things, hopes all things, endures all things."

Devotional:

God's love is enduring and steadfast. It perseveres through our trials, hardships, and challenges. It never gives up or loses faith.

Bearing All Things:

What does this mean, and how can we practically live this out daily? Bearing all things in unconditional love means being willing to carry the burdens (everyone has emotional wounds and healing to be done) and challenges of others without judgment or resentment (everyone is in the process of growth, including you and me).

We can practice this by cultivating empathy for others and seeking to understand their struggles and challenges without dismissing, minimizing, or judging them.

Someone once said that if you were raised in the exact circumstances and conditions others were, you would make the same decisions they have made. That stuck with me because it is the truth. We tend to judge others based on our actions but we were not reared in the same circumstances. It may be helpful to do some introspection here and see if having a judgmental attitude arises from pride and feeling superior to others. In this state, it is not possible to love unconditionally. If you are judging, you are not loving. To have empathy for what someone is experiencing, you can practice active listening (with no intentions of "fixing" them or defensively responding). Try putting yourself in the other person's shoes while offering them support, encouragement, and practical assistance if they ask you to.

Cultivate patience. This is essential in bearing all things. Unconditional love is patient (**1 Corinthians 13**). We have opportunities every day to learn this act of love.

I am usually impatient when I only think of myself and my own needs (selfishness) and not what is in the best interest of others. I get many opportunities daily, especially on my job, and some days, I fail miserably. Still, I am thankful that I am aware of when this is happening and have the choice to change directions.

Our scripture verse also tells us that love believes all things. This does not mean being gullible to believe everything that people say. It is about believing all things in love, which involves maintaining trust, optimism, and thinking of the best in others with confidence. How can we practically live this out, especially if those we have loved and trusted have proven to be unreliable? For me, this has not been easy, but I have decided not to "bleed on others who have not cut me."

This saying implies doing the work of emotional healing so as not to take that "baggage" into other relationships and view others through the lens of unhealed wounds.

Sometimes, the new relationships in our lives pay for what others have done. This is giving an automatic death sentence to new relationships, be it in your personal or professional lives. Heal so you can cleanse the lens in which you view the world, assuming positive intent. How can we do this?

We should approach interactions by giving others the benefit of the doubt and refraining from jumping to negative conclusions. Instead of assuming all that can go wrong mindset, how about approaching situations thinking of all that can go right? Instead of assuming someone has ill intent towards you because they do not do things according to your preferences, how about thinking that they are having good thoughts towards you? We also do this with God when we have sinned or fallen short of doing what is right. At times, we do not have the correct perspective of God's unconditional love towards us.

In that case, we may think He is out to get us, delighting in punishing us when we mess up.

Jeremiah 29:11 reminds us that the plans and thoughts God has towards us are for good and not for evil. Think about that. God has good thoughts towards us. So, let us practice giving others the benefit of the doubt and refrain from rushing to negative conclusions.

We can also learn to believe all things in love by building trust through consistency and demonstrating reliability and integrity in our interactions with others that foster an environment of trust. Follow through on commitments and be transparent and honest while acting in ways that reinforce trust and belief in others. Encouraging and expressing faith in others can profoundly impact our lives, the receiver and the giver. This can strengthen both individuals' sense of self-worth and capability.

I have had the blessings of having someone believe in me and the opportunity to encourage and believe in others when no one else did. It has dramatically impacted my life and changed the trajectory of my journey for the better.

People need cheerleaders to believe in them when they cannot believe in themselves. The cheerleader could be a spouse, a child, a friend, a coworker, or a stranger. Everyone needs someone to believe in and love them. Be that person.

Let us look at the next aspect of what unconditional love looks like. The scripture says that love hopes in all things. I have been in circumstances where all hope was lost in relationships and professional and family lives. You may be in a dire situation where you feel all hope is lost. I encourage you, like I too, was encouraged in past circumstances.

1 Corinthians 13 says, "Faith, hope, and love are the three greatest virtues on earth." We can have or try to attain many things in life, but we need these three to accomplish everything. To hope is to have an optimistic and enduring outlook for the future, even in adversity or challenges.

I know people who are living with progressively debilitating diseases and have challenges in maintaining hope in situations like these. I sometimes have challenges, but I must ensure I have the correct way of thinking about my situations. So, to refocus and return to my core, I go to the Source of all hope. **Lamentations 3:21-23** says, "But this I call to mind, and therefore I have hope. The steadfast love of the Lord never ceases; His mercies never end; they are new every morning; great is Your faithfulness."

Jeremiah, the prophet, expressed these words when he was in an emotionally dark place (it even sounds like depression if you read the entire chapter). He was first focusing on his circumstances, which were real and dire.

The more Jeremiah lamented his circumstances, the more hope he lost that his situation would end well. After he stopped and "called to mind," he shifted his focus from the problem to the problem solver.

He reminded himself of who he belonged to and who was on his side. This is the same **Jeremiah** who quoted one of my favorite scriptures in chapter **29:11**. Hope gives us the resilience to embrace challenges and setbacks as opportunities for growth and learning, fostering a hopeful mindset. Sometimes, we must stop and "call to mind," encourage ourselves, and remember where our hope comes from.

Hope helps us to bounce back from difficulties with determination and strength. **Hebrews 6:19** says, "We have this hope as an anchor for the soul, firm and secure."

Here are some more amazing scriptures to commit to memory so you can "call to mind" when you need them. **1 Peter 1:3** tells us we have a "...New birth (new beginning) in a LIVING hope through the resurrection of Jesus Christ..."

Job 11:18 reminds us that we will be secure because there is hope. We will look at ourselves and rest in safety.

Proverbs 13:12 says, "Hope deferred makes the heart sick..."

Romans 5:5: "And hope does not put us to shame, because God's love has been poured into our hearts, through His Holy Spirit, who has been given to us." There is hope for now and for the future. **Romans 15:13** says, "May the God of hope fill you with all joy and peace as you trust in Him, so that you may overflow with hope by the power of the Holy Spirit."

Titus 2:13 says, "While we wait for the blessed hope – the appearing of the glory of our great God and Savior, Jesus Christ."

The final scripture,**1 Corinthians 13:7**, tells us that true love endures all things. This involves being steadfast, persevering, and resilient in facing challenges and difficulties. How can we practically live this out in our daily lives? We can give our unwavering support to those going through a difficult time, standing with them through the highs and lows of life by being present and offering encouragement for their best interest.

We can give the gift of forgiveness, which is a powerful expression of enduring love.

Endurance in love often requires letting go of past hurts and grievances. This can profoundly impact our lives and those with whom we interact, our relationships, and our communities, fostering an environment of love, understanding, and support. Today, let us reflect on the enduring nature of God's love and how it calls us to love others similarly. May we be reminded of the importance of perseverance and commitment in our relationships, choosing to love and support others even when difficult.

Continue with this devotional, exploring different aspects of God's unconditional love each day and providing space for reflection, prayer, and growth in understanding and experiencing this incredible love. Allow God's love to shape and transform your life, and may you become a vessel of His love to those around you.

Reflection:

Consider times when God's love has brought you comfort and strength in difficult times. How does His enduring love inspire you to love others? Reflect on any relationships or situations where you must persevere or show commitment. Pray for grace and strength to endure and love unconditionally, as God does.

Prayer:

Gracious God, thank You for Your enduring love. Please help us bear, believe, hope, and endure all things in our relationships. Grant us the perseverance to love unconditionally and to stand firm in our commitments. Fill our hearts with Your steadfast love so that we may reflect Your enduring nature.

In Jesus' Name. Amen.

Debra Enile Armand

Reflection/Note-taking

_____

_____

_____

_____

_____

Reflection/Note-taking

_____

_____

_____

_____

_____

Day 16

Rediscovering True Love

Scripture: **1 John 4:16**: "And so we know and rely on the love God has for us. God is love. Whoever lives in love, lives in God, and God in them."

Devotional:

Today, we embark on a beautiful journey of rediscovering true love – the unconditional love of God. In a world often filled with conditional love and its expectations, it is essential to remember that we are loved by a God who never changes and always embraces us with unending grace. We have a foundation to build and grow from as our starting point. We will fail in relationships in every sphere of life if we continue to define and develop love from a humanistic perspective. As this book is entitled, this is a journey worth beginning and continuing.

Our entire earthly existence is to learn these foundational truths.

I have seen in my own life and the lives of those around me, and I dare say in the world, the futile efforts in defining love from our own experiences, which is always conditional and transactional. We have all learned to love this way, but God, in His infinite mercy, guides us to the Truth, which will set us free. I, like you, am a sojourner. I have learned only a minute portion of the vastness of this incredible love that has been offered and is available to us daily.

Our highest educational systems have taught us many wonderful things and have produced outstanding individuals who have done so much to make our world a better place to live in, except in teaching us how to love correctly. We will not get this essence if we bypass the Creator of Love, God the Father, God the Son, and God the Holy Spirit.

Marriages fail because two people try their best to love each other the only way they know how.

111

Countries are at war because, at the bottom line, leaders have no brotherly love and, therefore, cannot love their enemies or think of the best interests of others. We fight, squabble, hold grudges, rob, steal, and kill each other because we have no love for ourselves or humanity.

James 4:1-3 gives us a great picture of a loveless world in which we now live and participate. It says, "What leads to wars, quarrels, and conflicts among you? Do they not come from your desires that wage war in your (bodily) members (fighting for control over you)? You are jealous and covet (what others have) and your lust goes unfulfilled; so, you murder. You are envious and cannot obtain (the object of your envy); so, you fight and battle.

You do not have because you do not ask (it of God). You ask (God for something) and do not receive it, because you ask with the wrong motives (out of selfishness or with an unrighteous agenda), so that (when you get what you want) you may spend it on your (hedonistic) desires."

112

Now, this is a mouthful to reflect, ponder, and meditate upon. Mother Teresa once said, "If you want to change the world, go home and love your family." I say if you want to change the world, go back to **Matthew 22:37-40**. Learn to know and love God with your whole heart, soul, body, and mind. Then, you will be able to love your neighbor because you have learned your identity in Christ and now see and love yourself the way God sees and loves you. This is our foundation for building a house of love that will stand the test and trials of time and last through all eternity.

GOD IS LOVE. **1 John 4:16** says that whoever lives in love lives in God and God in him. Here is another moment to pause and ponder. Let us stop and meditate upon what this powerful Truth is telling us here. I do not know about you, but I desire this more than the air I breathe. Why is this journey with God worth every painful transformation in my life? **1 Corinthians 2:9** states a significant reason for us.

113

"But just as it is written (in scripture), things which the eye has not seen and the ear has not heard, and which have not entered the heart of man, all that God has prepared for those who love Him (who hold Him in affectionate reverence, who obey Him, and who gratefully recognize the benefits that He has bestowed)." There are no words in Webster's dictionary to put together sentences to describe what my heart and mind can conceive of how much God loves you and me. The most imaginative person on the face of this earth cannot conceive what God has prepared and has in store for those who love Him.

Take a moment to reflect on this truth: God's love for you knows no bounds. His love is not based on your performance, circumstances, or flaws but is pure, unwavering, and freely given. Pause and let that sink in. We learn what it means to love ourselves and others through God's love. His love teaches us to extend grace, forgiveness, and compassion without conditions or expectations.

As we immerse ourselves in His love, we see others through His lens – with kindness, understanding, and acceptance. Today's challenge is to let go of any preconceived notions of what love should look like and surrender to God's definition of love. Open your heart to receive His unconditional love, allowing it to fill every corner and overflow into your relationships, actions, and words. Rather than seeking validation from others, seek affirmation in God's love for you. Remind yourself daily that you are fearfully and wonderfully made and that your worth is rooted in your identity as a beloved child of God. Embrace your imperfections, knowing that God's love does not depend on your performance but on His grace.

In your interactions with others, strive to love without conditions. Offer understanding and forgiveness, even when it may be challenging. Remember that true love is not about what you can receive but about what you can give.

As you extend love without judgment, you reflect God's heart and desire for all His children.

Reflect and Respond:

1. Spend time today reflecting on God's unconditional love for you. Journal any thoughts or feelings that arise as you ponder on this truth.

2. Choose an act of love to practice today without any expectation of receiving anything in return. Let it reflect God's unconditional love for you and others.

3. Share your experience of God's unconditional love with someone you trust. Encourage them to embrace this love and discover its power in their lives.

Remember, true love is found in God's unwavering and unconditional love for us. May you continue to rediscover and experience this love in new and profound ways each day.

<u>Prayer:</u>

God, Abba, my Father, thank you for loving me unconditionally. Help me to fully comprehend the depths of Your love and let it transform my heart. Teach me to extend grace, forgiveness, and compassion to those around me, just as You do for me. May Your love flow through me in all my relationships, expressing Your unconditional love to the world.

In Jesus' Name, Amen.

Debra Enile Armand

Reflection/Note-taking

_____

_____

_____

_____

_____

Reflection/Note-taking

_____

_____

_____

_____

_____

Day 17

Experiencing Love in Relationships

Scripture: **1 Peter 4:8**: "Above all, love each other deeply because love covers over a multitude of sins."

Devotional:

Someone said, "Love is not love until you give it away." When we think about love, our minds often gravitate towards romantic relationships. While romantic love is undoubtedly a beautiful aspect of our lives, it is crucial to recognize that love extends far beyond just that. Love is meant to be embraced and experienced in all relationships – with family, friends, coworkers, and strangers. If we continue to view love as some abstract feeling we desperately try to attain, what happens when the "feelings" are no longer there? We see the devastation of that all around us in our world today. Feelings change, sometimes daily. Unconditional love is spiritual, not concocted by our minds or the gods we have created by our hands.

Love is from the only true God, the Creator and Source. Someone once said we are not humans trying to have a spiritual experience. We are spiritual beings having a human experience. Love produces a feeling, but love is not the feeling. Think about that for a minute.

To experience love in all our relationships, we start with the Source and get plugged into the Source. This is more than a one-and-done experience. We in a world today where we want a quick fix, an antidote to take and run with in our strength. It does not work that way. Jesus taught us a fundamental fact in **John 15:4-5**. He said if we remain in Him and He in us, just as no branch can bear fruit by itself without remaining in the vine, neither can we unless we remain in Him (bear fruit-manifested evidence of our faith). He is the Vine; we are the branches.

The one who remains in Him and He in them bears much fruit, for apart from Him (that is cut off from vital union with Him), we can do nothing.

It is moment by moment, day by day, of making decisions to follow Him rather than our selfish desires. Love, we will see, is selfless, and we cannot do this without the supernatural power of God's Spirit living and moving in and through us. It is our daily decisions that determine whether we choose love or pain. When we follow our selfish ways, the result brings pain to us and others.

Let us look at **Galatians 5: 16, 17, 19-23.**

[16]But I say, walk habitually in the (Holy) Spirit (seek Him and be responsive to His guidance) and then you will certainly not carry out the desire of the sinful nature (which responds impulsively without regard for God and His percepts).

[17] For the sinful nature has its desire which is opposed to the (Holy) Spirit and the (desire of the) Spirit opposes the sinful nature; for these (two, the sinful nature and the Spirit) are in direct opposition to each other (continually in conflict), so that you do not (always) do whatever (good things) you want to do.

[19] Now the practices of the sinful nature are clear: they are sexual immorality, impurity, sensuality (total irresponsibility, lack of self-control),

[20]idolatry, sorcery, hostility, strife, jealousy, fits of anger, disputes, dissensions, factions (that promote heresies),

[21] envy, drunkenness, riotous behavior, and other things like these. I warn you beforehand, just as I did previously, that those who practice such things, will not inherit the kingdom of God. (I believe in this earth or in the life to come).

Verses 22-23 tell us how our life can be if we abide in and stay responsive to Christ. "But the fruit of the Spirit (the result of His Presence within us) is love (unselfish concern for others), joy, (inner) peace, patience (not the ability to wait, but how we act while waiting), kindness, goodness, faithfulness, gentleness, self-control. Against such there is no law."

Some scripture versions say the "works of the flesh" and the "fruits of the Spirit." This is not lost on me. The works or actions of human nature will result in all described above. That may be the reason some may say, I cannot do this unconditional love thing. It is only "natural" for me to get jealous, angry, etc. at times. You are correct.

Sinful human nature will do those things. But we are not left alone or helpless to maneuver in this world and our relationships.

The Bible assures us that if we continue to abide and connect to the Vine (Jesus Christ in the power of His Holy Spirit), we will produce fruit of love, joy, peace, patience, kindness, etc. As a budding gardener, I have learned this principle and am reminded whenever I pick fruits or vegetables. The fruit depends upon the tree; the branches cannot produce fruit independently. If you grow grapes, you will see the same.

There would be no fruits or vegetables without the vine or the tree. Therefore, we will not produce SUSTAINABLE characteristics that will last without Christ. We look for these in relationships, but we must work on ourselves to have what we desire in others.

To have genuine and unfailing love for one another, because love covers a multitude of sins (it overlooks unkindness and unselfishly seeks the best for others), we must be connected and stay connected to the Source. We are not just checking off a box of religious activities but making the daily, moment-by-moment decisions to follow the instructions of God's Holy Spirit because He will give us the power and strength to do so.

This type of love will cover (extend over an area, put something on top of or in front of something to protect it) a multitude of sins for those we love. It is not intended to enable nor expose their behavior for our selfish gain. It is not about getting others to support us versus them.

When we genuinely love others, we are willing and able to overlook or forgive their faults and shortcomings. Isn't this what Christ does for us daily? This love is transformative and healing. We extend the same healing love to others that has healed us.

Through these lenses, we see more compassionately the positive qualities of others rather than being consumed and focused on their mistakes and imperfections.

Love can now see past their "multitude of sins," empathize, and offer grace, forgiveness, understanding, and acceptance. We all have flaws and failings. We all need the healing power of unconditional love. By loving each other deeply despite our shortcomings, we participate in the redemptive work of reconciliation and healing in our families, communities, and world. This is the love that God extends to each one of us and has asked us to offer this to others, recognizing our shared humanity as we respond in compassion and understanding.

The tremendous benefit of loving others unconditionally is that we impact those around us and experience personal growth and spiritual enrichment, cultivating a loving and forgiving heart. God calls us to love one another deeply, just as He has loved us.

Today, let us focus on discovering how to love wholeheartedly in our relationships. When we love without conditions, we create an environment where people feel safe, valued, and supported. We become a reflection of God's unconditional love, specifically designed to cover many sins and heal broken relationships. Reflect on the relationships in your life. Are there any areas where love may be lacking? Are there grudges you are holding onto, inhibiting the flow of love? Bring these concerns before God, asking for His wisdom and guidance in loving others more deeply.

Remember that loving others sincerely does not mean compromising your boundaries or enabling harmful behavior.

It means setting healthy standards while still loving and supporting those around you. Sometimes, loving someone altogether means speaking the truth with gentleness and compassionately offering guidance.

As you navigate your relationships, be intentional about expressing love through words and actions. Offer a listening ear to a friend in need. Speak kind and affirming words to a family member. Extend grace to a coworker who made a mistake. Show compassion to a stranger who may be going through a challenging time.

Reflect and Respond:

1. Take a few moments to evaluate your relationships. Write down some steps to demonstrate love more deeply in those relationships.

2. Reflect on a time when someone loved you unconditionally, even when you did not deserve it. How did that impact you? Consider how you can extend the same unconditional love to others.

3. Practice forgiveness today. Is there someone you need to forgive?

Ask God to give you the strength and willingness to let go of any grudges or resentment, choosing to extend love instead.

In every relationship, may you embrace the call to love sincerely and wholeheartedly. May your actions speak louder than words, reflecting God's unconditional love.

Prayer:

Loving God, teach me to love others deeply, just as You have loved me. Help me to extend grace, forgiveness, and understanding in my relationships. Show me when to set healthy standards and guide me in discerning how to express love in each situation. May I be a vessel of Your love as I choose to remain in Your love and You in me, bringing healing and restoration to the relationships in my life.

In Jesus' Name, Amen.

Reflection/Note-taking

_____

_____

_____

_____

_____

Day 18

Love in Action

Scripture: **1 John 3:18**: "Dear children, let us not love with words or speech but with actions and in truth."

Devotional:

Love is often expressed by saying "I love you," offering compliments, or encouraging words. While words hold power, it is in our actions that love genuinely comes alive. Love is not just something we say; it is something we do; it is who we become. This has been and continues to be one of the most challenging aspects of this journey: Love in action. It is not about my actions demonstrating God's love to others but about being brutally honest with the motives coming from my heart and core. We have learned that love is not love unless it is selfless, unconditional, and seeking the best interest of others. This is easier said than done in our strength.

I am tested with this moment-by-moment, day-by-day. The testing is not tortuous, but utilizing the power of choice and self-awareness helps me decide if I am seeking my selfish interest for my desired outcomes or genuinely seeking the best interest of others. Opportunities for transformation are all around me, including my relationships with my children, extended family, coworkers, employees, patients, the cashier at the checkout counter, and the intimate relationship I desire in my life. The last is one of the most difficult to put on paper. I believe anyone can "act" lovingly, but people can "feel" when it is not genuine because love is spiritual.

When we love like God, the Spirit of God is in the love we give to others. That is what people "feel." It is not something we can conjure up in a humanistic way. The spirit in the love of God connects people deeply, and that is what God is teaching me with the one man that I thought I loved for a very long time (in what I knew love was at the time).

My lack of the Spirit of God selfishly drove my conditional love for him. It was about how he "made" me feel, how I wanted him to be. In my mind, I built the illusion that being with this prince charming would make me happy. All the fairy tales we grew up with played a part in us placing those unrealistic expectations upon others. It was all about what he could do for me emotionally. It was conditional.

As I took responsibility for my emotional healing, growth, and stability, God began to reveal to me (through His love for me) that what I called love was not love. Thus began this journey of learning to love another selflessly. And this gentleman did not actively participate in this discovery. God used him profoundly in this part of my journey (unbeknownst to him). For example, I became very aware of the times I communicated with him to get a desired response that would benefit me. I decided not to contact him if this was my motive.

I had to deal with and get rid of the emotional junk food to which I had become accustomed.

It is like a person with an addiction that keeps going back to drugs or alcohol when they do not want to deal with their reality and use something or someone as a temporary escape. So, I am learning not to contact him if my motives are selfishly driven. Learning to love others with their best interests at heart has taught me that selfless love removes expectations and conditions we place on others as recipients of our love. Unconditional love has no expectations for selfish rewards. We do not give love to get something back in return.

We offer love to others, and that is it! I told you this was not easy, but God has not left us alone in this journey. God, by His Spirit, gives us His power and strength to love like this. It is not something I can do or sustain in my own strength. Some might think this is crazy; this cannot be done. I agree; humanly speaking, it cannot. But I am a living testimony that God can love this way through us.

Those who have been courageous to take this journey have the same testimony. I am not the first to journey this way with the Lord, and certainly not the last. People's lives have been drastically changed and continue to change upon learning these principles.

Loving another human without placing selfish expectations and conditions upon the relationship is healing and powerful. In regards to the aforementioned gentleman, I am learning that since this love is seeking his best interest, it also means that if he makes his choice to be with someone he sees as his life partner and that is what God wants for him, I can be happy for him because his best interest does not have to include me. This has been revolutionary for me.

Knowing that I am already loved beyond my comprehension (by God) contributed to bringing me to this place, and no man can love me like God does. That is my source of love. The other factor was believing that I am unconditionally loved and already chosen (by God); therefore, I am not waiting for a man to choose me.

Love in action, in a relationship, gives each party the freedom of choice, and by seeking the other's best interest, love is no longer selfishly driven. I can love this man by wanting the best for him, even if that does not include me.

He is free to choose his path, as I have chosen mine. This is the first time in my life I have been able to love this way. It is the most powerful journey I have taken: to love others the way God loves me, to lay aside my selfish desires for the betterment of another.

Has this been easy? Not by a long shot. Constantly deciding to love this way when my human instincts desire the opposite is evidence of God's healing power. God gives me His grace and strength at each opportunity. Just recently, I became discouraged with what I saw as the need for more progress in our journey. In my mind, he was not doing the things I wanted him to do, moving as quickly as I wanted him to. Do you see the selfish pattern?

As I lay in bed early one chilly morning, contemplating just giving up on this man, the Lord reminded me of what unconditional love in action was about. He whispered in my heart, "Debra, you can walk away and sever all communication, but it will be because you did not get your way in your time. That is your choice. But are you willing to lay aside all of what you desire and continue to maintain a presence in his life, if I only wanted you to be My Voice, to be a friend that will be there when he faces his challenges, so you can remind him of how much I love him, even if you never get to be his life partner?"

As the large streams of hot tears formed a puddle below my cheeks on my pillow that morning, I decided to stay put so God could use me as His voice in the life of another. This is my love in action, not just saying "I love you," but meaning it through actions. **1 John 3:18** reminds us that love is not merely about speaking kind and loving words. Love requires action and truth. It is in our actions that we demonstrate the love that God has shown us.

Jesus Christ (God) became a man to teach and demonstrate what love in action looks like. He is our example, and His Holy Spirit is our Helper. Think about that. God, in Christ Jesus, walked out the human experience of love through the power of God's Spirit in Him to show us that, with God, all things are possible. What seems impossible with man is possible with God's power in us.

Today, let us examine our actions in our relationships. Are we actively demonstrating love through our behavior? Do our actions align with the love we proclaim with our words? It is easy to get caught up in expressing love through words alone, but true love requires us to go beyond verbal affirmation.

Take a moment to reflect on your daily interactions. Are there opportunities to show love through small acts of kindness? It could be as simple as helping a coworker with a task, making a meal for a friend in need, or even offering a smile to a stranger.

These small acts may seem insignificant, but they have the power to make a significant impact on the lives of others. Consider the unconditional love God has shown you. How can you extend that same love to those around you? Love in action involves stepping outside of our comfort zones and going the extra mile for others. It requires sacrificial giving, putting others' needs before our own. As you go about your day, be intentional about demonstrating love through your actions. Look for opportunities to serve and bless others. Ask God to guide you and give you a heart of compassion and selflessness. Seek to show love not just in grand gestures but also in the small, everyday moments.

Reflect and Respond:

1. Consider one relationship where you can love through your actions. Write down three specific actions to show love in that relationship.

2. Reflect on when someone's actions spoke louder than their words and demonstrated love to you. How did that impact you?

How can you emulate that same kind of love in your relationships?

3. Pay attention to the small, everyday moments where you can show love through your actions. It could be something as simple as holding the door for someone or offering a listening ear. Be intentional about seizing those opportunities to demonstrate love.

Remember, love in action goes beyond words. It requires us to step out and show love through our behavior. May your actions reflect God's love, impacting those around you and drawing them closer to Him.

Prayer:

Heavenly Father, help me to love in action and Your truth. Show me how to extend love through my deeds and behavior. Open my eyes to the needs of those around me, and give me the strength and courage to step beyond my comfort zone to serve and bless others.

May my actions reflect Your love and bring glory to Your name.

In Jesus' Name, Amen.

Reflection/Note-taking

_____

_____

_____

_____

_____

_____

Reflection/Note-taking

_____

_____

_____

_____

_____

Day 19

Love in Service

Scripture: **Mark 10:45**: "For even the Son of Man did not come to be served, but to serve, and to give his life as a ransom for many."

Devotional:

The call to love in service can be counter-cultural in a world that often encourages us to pursue self-interest and personal gain. But as followers of Christ, we are called to emulate His example of selfless service and sacrifice. Jesus Himself declared that He did not come to be served but to serve. Operating in a Spirit-led behavior of unconditional love can be challenging for me. Sometimes, it feels nearly impossible when dealing with various people who have never experienced unconditional love and unleash the furor of their emotional pain and trauma upon anyone in their path. In today's age of continuously serving the public, this can be emotionally depleting, especially if you are not plugged into the Source from which you can be replenished with love.

Jesus was and is the epitome of living in a fleshly body, empowered by the Holy Spirit to unconditionally serve all humanity in love, even the ones who despised, persecuted, and ill-treated Him. In **Mark 10:45**, Jesus demonstrates the essence of love through His willingness to give His life as a ransom for many. He set aside personal comfort and desires to serve the greater purpose of redemption, salvation, and restoration. His ultimate act of service reveals the depth of His love for us. You may say that is Jesus, God in the flesh. He can do that, but I cannot.

Then you missed the point that He was born in the flesh and felt all the same things we experienced. The same Holy Spirit of God empowered him (as man) to help Him (as Savior) accomplish His destiny on earth.

The same Holy Spirit that lived in and through Him, Who raised Him from the dead, is available to you and me today to do what Jesus did on the earth and so much more.

And you are correct. We cannot do this in our strength, but the Helper is available to us if we receive Him. As we strive to love as Jesus loved, let us embrace the call to serve others. Service is an expression of love in action, where we put the needs of others above our own. It is an opportunity to extend God's love and grace to those around us, just as Jesus did.

Serving others can take various forms. It can be as simple as lending a helping hand or offering a listening ear. It can involve volunteering in a local charity, fostering relationships with those in need, or taking on tasks that others may find burdensome. The key is to approach serving with humility, seeking to bless others and meeting their needs without looking for anything in return.

Today, reflect on the areas where you can practice love in service. Are there opportunities within your family, community, or workplace where you can extend a helping hand or offer your time and resources?

147

Ask God to reveal those areas to you and give you the strength and willingness to serve. Remember, faithful service is not about seeking recognition or personal gain. It is about sacrificing ourselves for the well-being and upliftment of others. It is a way to tangibly express the love of God and reflect His character to those around us.

Reflect and Respond:

1. Take a moment to evaluate your heart and motives when serving others. Are there any areas of self-interest or seeking recognition that you need to surrender to God? Ask Him to help you cultivate a heart of selfless service.

2. Consider specific ways you can serve others in your daily life. It could be volunteering at a local soup kitchen, offering to help a neighbor with their yard work, or being intentional about listening and supporting a friend going through a difficult time. Write down three practical ways you can extend love to others through service.

3. Look for opportunities to practice love in service throughout your day. Be attentive to the needs of those around you and be willing to step in and offer your help. Remember that even small acts of service can significantly impact someone's life.

As you follow in Jesus' footsteps, may your heart be filled with God's unconditional love, motivating you to serve others with humility and grace. May your actions be a testament to His love and bring hope and healing to those in need.

Prayer:

Dear Heavenly Father, thank you for the example of Jesus, who came to serve and give His life for us. Help me to embrace the call to love in service, putting the needs of others before my own. Open my eyes to the opportunities to serve those around me, and give me a heart of humility and compassion. Guide me in my actions so that they may reflect Your love and bring glory to Your name.

In Jesus' Name, Amen.

Day 20

Love is Patient and patience has no timeline

1 Corinthians 13:4: "Love is patient (long suffering) and serene; love is kind and thoughtful."

Devotional:

Another way we can look at patience is through the lens of long-suffering or endurance. It is not only waiting but how we act while we wait. How do you respond when someone annoys you? Do you seek or desire revenge or take revenge when the opportunity arises? It could be in "small" ways, like gossiping about them or trying to assassinate their character in the eyes of others, for example. I know I have. Now, I must be aware of how my thoughts and judgments of someone affect how I view and respond to them so I can use those opportunities to work on myself. The Greek word for patience comes from two words that mean "long-tempered."

This means you are slow to become angry and can endure personal wrongs without retaliating or seeking revenge.

Being patient shows up in the form of empathy toward others' shortcomings, imperfections, flaws, and differences. Being patient gives others room to make mistakes, giving them time to change without being overly critical of them.

I confess that patience was one of my weaknesses. I was too impatient. Intellectually, I knew it was evident that I needed to love "better." I tried repeatedly and failed this love test every time. I could be patient until someone "hit my last nerve." I am smiling as I write this because I know countless of you will resonate with this.

I lingered in getting into this day of devotion because I did not want to only give all the biblical scriptures on being patient without consistently knowing and implementing this trait.

So, when I failed yet another test, I became impatient with myself about "knowing I should do better" and not losing my cool in trying circumstances. I lay in bed early in the morning, talking to God about this.

How can I write to others about this when I struggle in this area? God whispered in my heart, "My child, you have been struggling with this for so long because of your perspective of what love is, and you are trying to do this from your strength and your willpower. I have been teaching you that unconditional love is spiritual. It is My Spirit working in and through you. When you try to do this in your strength, you fail. Love is spiritual, so the byproduct of My love, patience, is also spiritual." Then, it hit me like a ton of bricks. Patience was always something I thought I had to do, instead of seeing that as I abide in God's love and His love abides in me, patience will be one of the fruit of His Spirit. It is a spiritual power.

I thank God that He has been so patient with me throughout the years and will continue to be patient with you and me. God's love causes us to be patient with others and ourselves as we are transformed in stages through life experiences and various chapters and seasons of our lives.

It will cause us to be patient in those problematic places as we await the Lord and His direction for our lives. It will cause us to be patient with loved ones working through their emotional pain in their journey and not "getting it" as quickly as we would like them to. It will cause us to be patient on the job when we want to advance and have been looked over time and again for that promotion. We will be patient because we know His love is patient, and He has the best plans for our lives because He unconditionally loves us.

So, my focus is not on what I need to do to become more patient but on continuing to learn and abide in this beautiful space of His unconditional love.

He will exhibit His love through me in the form of patience. God's love is patient; mine (conditional love) is not, and with His Holy Spirit living and working in me, patience will be one fruit that will be developed in me and can be gifted to others.

Reflect and Respond:

Take a moment to think about a time when someone showed you incredible patience. Think about how God has been patient with you throughout your life. Then, go a little further and look back at how He has been patient with the world since the creation of time. How does that make you feel? As you reflect on this, ask God to help you cultivate His love in your own heart, enabling you to respond with patience, empathy, and understanding toward others.

Prayer:

Heavenly Father, I confess that I often struggle with impatience. Please help me grow in Your love so I may demonstrate Your patience to those around me. Teach me to wait with grace and to extend understanding in challenging situations.

In Jesus' Name, Amen.

Reflection/Note-taking

Day 21

Love is Kind

1 Corinthians 13:4: "Love is patient (long-suffering) and serene; love is kind and thoughtful."

Devotional:

Love is described by action words, not lofty concepts or religious activities. Actions will consistently demonstrate God's unconditional love growing in us. **1 John 3:18** reminds us as believers, beloved by God, "Let us not love (merely in theory) with word or tongue (lip service), but in action and in truth (in practice and in sincerity, because practical acts of love are more than words)." True love produces action (fruit). I know most of us would like to characterize ourselves as loving people, so I would challenge all of us, me included, to compare our version of a loving person to the Source of Love, God Himself, in His Words here in the Bible.

Apostle Paul, the writer of 1 Corinthians 13, was teaching the church that love is the most superior spiritual gift.

We can all use our gifts and talents to better our world, but without love, it means nothing (**I Corinthians 13:1-3**).

I would rather love and be kind to others than have a PhD in bio-nuclear medicine and have no love in my heart. ***Kindness is patience in action.*** Kindness is a response to the thoughts and judgments we have and make of others. If our thoughts are unloving, our responses to others will be unloving. Jesus taught us in **Matthew 5:44,** "But I say to you, love (that is, unselfishly seek the best or higher good for) your enemies and pray for those who persecute you." **Verse 46**: "For if you love (only) those who love you, what reward do you have? Do not even the tax collectors do that?"

So, we have established that kindness is an act of love. It is easy to love those who love and agree with us, but this has been my struggle that I am growing through, loving those who persecute and harm my loved ones or myself.

How do I show kindness to my enemies- or people who behave unlovingly?

The difference maker for me on this journey of understanding what true love is like is in **verse 45,** which shows that I will be like my "Father in heaven; for He makes His sun rise on those who are evil and those who are good, and makes the rain fall on the righteous (those who are morally upright) and the unrighteous (the unrepentant, those who oppose Him)." **Verse 48** tells us, "You therefore will be perfect (growing into spiritual maturity both in mind and character, actively integrating godly values into your daily life) as your heavenly Father is perfect." Being kind to the unloving benefits them and you because you are not expecting anything in return. Jesus is our perfect example.

Reflection:

Can you think of times in your life when He has shown you kindness through the love of others? Think about a person in your life who may need kindness.

How can you show them love through acts of kindness today? Take a moment to pray and ask God to reveal opportunities for you to extend love and kindness to others.

Prayer:

Dear Lord, You are the epitome of kindness. Teach me to be kind to others, especially when it may be difficult. Fill my heart with Your love so I can overflow with kindness, reflecting Your character and bringing comfort and joy to those I encounter.

In Jesus' Name, Amen.

Day 22

Love does Not Envy

1 Corinthians 13:4: "Love is not jealous or envious."

Devotional:

Numerous scriptures in the Bible advise us not to envy evildoers because envy can lead to destructive behavior and dissatisfaction. Envying evildoers who practice and delight in wrongdoing can lead us away from righteous living and toward harmful actions. The Bible encourages us to focus on our paths and trust God's ultimate justice and fairness. What I realize more and more the longer I travel this path is that everything we do comes down to what we believe and our faith, which results from how much we trust in God, His Word, and His Ways. This is a result of how much we believe He unconditionally loves us. We cannot trust, believe in, or have faith in God if we do not honestly believe He loves us beyond what we can think or imagine.

When this reality becomes a part of our every being, we will trust that His ways and the path he has for us are for our good. So, let us look at envy. Can you be envious and jealous of someone and still love them? What is envy? How can it destabilize individuals, relationships, communities, and even nations? Then, we will discuss the solution and how we can practically apply a different perspective while cultivating godly habits to counteract envy in our everyday lives.

- **Envy** is the **emotion** that arises when a person lacks another person's quality, achievements, or possessions and either desires it or wishes the other person lacked it. Feelings of inferiority, longing, and resentment characterize this emotion.

- **Jealousy** involves the fear of losing something or someone that one considers their own (their possession), which is often accompanied by feelings of insecurity, anxiety, and fear of loss.

161

- **Coveting** pertains to an intense desire to possess something or someone that belongs to another, with an intense yearning to acquire it beyond admiration and appreciation. There is a focused longing for specific possessions, attributes, or circumstances that belong to another.

The difference between these three is that envy is directed at someone else's possessions or attributes. It is a reaction to a perceived lack compared to someone else that could involve resentment. Jealousy is about the threat of losing something (or someone) to someone else, which is rooted in fear and can react in protectiveness or possessiveness. Covetousness is the strong desire to possess something that belongs to another.

The Lord instructs us not to be jealous or envious of others so we can avoid the negative consequences of these emotions if left unchecked. His instructions show the importance of following a godly path.

This is God's unconditional love for us, to keep us off a destructive path that not only affects our lives but can affect the lives of many others. In **Proverbs 14:30,** envy is described as rottenness to the bones, illustrating this emotion's destructive impact on our well-being.

Proverbs 14:30 is a profound piece of wisdom literature that offers insight into the nature of inner peace and its impact on one's well-being. The verse reads, "A heart at peace gives life to the body, but envy rots the bones."

This verse, simple yet deep, touches on two fundamental human emotions: contentment and envy, setting them in stark contrast to each other in relation to health and wellness. The first part of the verse, "A heart at peace gives life to the body," suggests that inner tranquility and contentment are not just emotional or spiritual states but positively affect physical health. The phrase "gives life to the body" implies vitality, health, and longevity.

Peace of mind and contentment with one's circumstances can lead to a healthier, more fulfilling life. This part of the verse echoes the well-documented notion that stress, anxiety, and unrest can harm physical health. At the same time, peace and contentment can enhance well-being.

The second part of the verse, "But envy rots the bones," addresses the destructive nature of envy. Envy is described as something that 'rots the bones,' a graphic depiction of deep, internal decay. This metaphor underscores the insidiousness of envy, suggesting it can undermine one's health from the inside out, just as rot would weaken the structure it invades. Using "bones" emphasizes the depth of the impact, as bones are often associated with structure, support, and inner strength. Thus, envy is portrayed as not merely an unpleasant emotion but a potent force that can erode one's foundational well-being.

Proverbs 14:30 highlights the choice between peace and envy and the consequences of each by contrasting these two states of being.

The verse encourages the cultivation of a peaceful heart, implying that such an attitude towards life is beneficial not just for one's emotional or spiritual state but also for one's physical health. At the same time, it warns against the toxic influence of envy, which can lead to both emotional turmoil and physical degradation.

Proverbs 14:30 powerfully reminds us of the interconnectedness of the spirit, mind, and body. It emphasizes the importance of cultivating inner peace and contentment as a way of life, not just for spiritual or emotional reasons but for one's overall health.

Furthermore, it underscores the destructive potential of envy, not only as a moral failing but as a real danger to physical well-being. In its brevity and wisdom, this verse sums up a profound truth about the human condition.

It offers guidance for a healthier, more harmonious life.

I hope you are beginning to see that loving others the way God loves us leads us away from a path that ultimately destroys us, first internally and then manifests externally.

James 3:14-16 –The apostle Paul warns against envy and strife, stating that they lead to disorder and every evil practice. In today's world that often values material wealth, success, and status, envy, and jealousy can easily take root in our hearts, leading to self-centeredness and lack of contentment, resulting in disorder and sinful behavior that affects the innocent, our families, communities, and society. James warns against the bitterness of envy and the chaos it can bring into one's life. Envy can also be subtle. Let us ask the Holy Spirit to show us our hearts and unveil the subtle areas we are unaware of so that we will not be deceived and find ourselves with "rotted bones."

The following scriptures further inform us of the damaging consequences of these feelings if left untreated:

Exodus 20:17 lists the 10th commandment given to the Israelites, which prohibits coveting as it harms one's spiritual well-being.

In **Galatians 5:19-21**, we are warned of the acts of our sinful nature (the flesh), which list jealousy and envy among these destructive deeds and instruct us that those who engage in them will not inherit God's kingdom.

Proverbs 24:1-2,19-20 instructs us, "Do not be envious of evil men, nor desire to be with them; For their minds plot violence, and their lips talk of trouble (for the innocent)." **Verses 19-20:** "Do not get upset because of evildoers, or be envious of the wicked. For there will be no future for the evil man; The lamp of the wicked will be put out."

Proverbs 23:17-18: "Do not let your heart envy sinners (who live godless lives and have no hope of salvation) But (continue to) live in the (reverent, worshipful) fear of the Lord, day by day."

Finally, in **Romans 13:13-14,** Paul encourages us to live in a manner that is free from jealousy and encourages embodying the teachings and character of Jesus Christ, which His Holy Spirit will help us with (one of His names is the Helper, the Paraclete, the Comforter, Advocate, the One who comes alongside us to help us on this life's journey).

When left unchecked, these destructive emotions can lead to wrongful behavior, such as destructive comparisons of ourselves to others and coveting what they have.

- This can result in feelings of inadequacy and resentment, leading to a desire to sabotage or harm others to elevate oneself.

- The harmful desire can be in our thoughts, words, and actions.

- One can justify harming others due to a distorted perception or rationale to obtain what is coveted.

- Empathy erodes when individuals are consumed by envy.

- They become increasingly indifferent to the impact of their actions on others or society.

- One can use manipulative or deceitful behavior or tactics to undermine others or to gain an advantage, such as gossiping, spreading false information, sabotaging relationships, or using other forms of manipulation to satisfy desires at the expense of others.

- Disregarding ethical boundaries and moral principles in pursuit of what others possess can manifest in dishonesty, theft, or other unethical actions.

- Self-destructive choices to compete with or hurt others, such as compromising personal values or engaging in risky behaviors, is another evidence of unchecked destructive emotions.

These examples convey the message that envy of those who choose to do evil can lead to fretting, spiritual unrest, and a departure from moral uprightness.

The Bible teaches that such envy can distract individuals from pursuing righteousness, ultimately leading to adverse outcomes. Instead, it encourages believers to focus on their faith and trust that God will finally bring justice and righteousness to all.

These verses underscore the importance of maintaining a steadfast and faithful spirit, even in the face of apparent success or prosperity enjoyed by those who engage in wrongdoing. The broader message is about the value of living by God's principles of unconditional love and not allowing envy to lead us astray from the path of righteousness and obedience.

We can avoid envying evildoers by practicing several vital principles outlined in the Bible and through thoughtful reflection.

Here are some of the ways:

1. Show Gratitude and Contentment:

Cultivate a spirit of gratitude for what one has by becoming aware of the loving-kindness of God **(Psalms 33:5, 89:1, Romans 2:4, Titus 3:4)**.

Find contentment in God's blessings to help mitigate feelings of envy. One of the significant marketing ploys used, is to bombard and encourages us to feel discontented with what we do have and envious of what we do not have or mostly do not need. To overcome envy, let us look at **1 Timothy 6:6-7**, which says, "But godliness (actually) is a source of great gain when accompanied by contentment (that contentment which comes from a sense of inner confidence based on the sufficiency of God).

For we have brought nothing into this world, so (it is clear that) we cannot take anything out of it, either." God's unconditional love teaches us to find contentment and gratitude in what we have rather than coveting what others possess. It encourages a shift in focus from longing for what others have to appreciating and being grateful for the blessings and gifts already present in one's life.

2. Focus on Personal Growth:

171

Engaging in continual self-improvement and spiritual growth can shift the focus from the actions of others to one's development. **Galatians 6:4-5** says, "Each one must (carefully) scrutinize his work (examining his actions, attitudes, and behaviors). Then, he can have the personal satisfaction and inner joy of doing something commendable without comparing himself to another, for every person will have to bear (with patience) his burden (of faults and shortcomings for which he alone is responsible)."

Taking personal responsibility for our own emotional and spiritual growth is very courageous.

This has been revolutionary for me. I stopped blaming others for the outcomes in my life spiritually, emotionally, financially, and physically. The longer I stayed in the 'victim' mentality, the less I progressed. My growth was my responsibility, not my husband, pastor, friends, work environment, children, past, or anything or anyone else. My life was my responsibility. I'll say it again. My life was my responsibility.

3. Avoid Comparisons:

Refraining from comparing one's life to the lives of others can prevent the development of envy. This is a big one because this is where you must be convinced and grounded in God's love for you. You are enough. God has made you enough. Your value is priceless.

2 Peter 1:3-4 teaches us that God's "Divine power has given us (absolutely) everything necessary for (a dynamic spiritual) life and godliness through personal knowledge of Him who has called us by His glory and excellence. He has given us His own precious and magnificent promises (of inexpressible value) so that we can escape from the immoral freedom in the world and become sharers of the divine nature."

God's unconditional love addresses the root of envy, jealousy, and covetousness by providing a sense of security and belonging.

It reaffirms everyone's worth and belovedness, alleviating the fear of loss and insecurity that fuels these destructive emotions. God's unconditional love offers a secure sense of identity and purpose that transcends external validation or comparison. This security reduces the need to covet what others have or feel threatened by their successes. Unconditional love embraces others without comparison or judgment.

In contrast, envy and jealousy stem from comparing oneself to others and feeling inadequate. Unconditional love celebrates individual uniqueness and value without the need for comparison.

Each person's journey is unique, and comparison can lead to dissatisfaction. **2 Corinthians 10:12** tells us not to have the audacity to put ourselves in the same class or compare ourselves with those who commend themselves. When people measure themselves and compare themselves with others, they lack wisdom and behave like fools.

4. Seek God's Guidance:

Seeking guidance from God through prayer and meditation on His Word can provide strength and clarity in resisting feelings of envy. Be honest with Him. He knows all our thoughts, feelings, and desires and can help us overcome them.

Go back to the scriptures, study and memorize them so they can counteract feelings of inadequacy when they arise until you are healed in this area. Hence, it is essential to get into a great Bible-believing church and engage in the study of God's Word.

5. Develop Compassion and Empathy:

Continually choosing to abide in God's love helps us develop compassion and empathy towards others, including those who engage in wrongdoing. This can help us foster a mindset of understanding rather than envy. God's unconditional love frees individuals from the trap of comparison and envy by emphasizing each person's worth and unique purpose.

It fosters a sense of self-worth and purpose independent of external possessions, attributes, or circumstances, thus reducing the tendency to compare and covet.

God's unconditional love nurtures empathy and compassion towards others, fostering a genuine concern for their well-being rather than viewing them as rivals or obstacles.

It encourages individuals to celebrate the successes and blessings of others without feeling threatened or envious.

One of my mentors, Pete Uglow (Restoringlove.com), said, "If we grew up in the same family, with the exact circumstances that others were raised in, we would make the same choices they made." Developing empathy for the life that someone was born into and the circumstances they faced in childhood that distorted their perception of themselves and the world around them is conducive to viewing them with compassion. It does not negate their adult responsibilities for their actions.

Still, it helps us see through their eyes, and we can help turn our lives around and theirs.

6. Trust in God's Justice:

God assures us that when we trust in His ultimate justice and righteousness, inappropriate actions and wrongdoings will not go unnoticed or unpunished. **Romans 12:19** says, "Beloved, never avenge yourself, but leave the way open for God's wrath (and His judicial righteousness) for it is written, 'Vengeance is Mine, I will repay,' says the Lord."

7. Limit Exposure:

Limit exposure to the actions and behaviors of those who engage in wrongdoing. This may involve avoiding certain media or social circles disproportionately highlighting such behavior. God's unconditional love provides ethical and moral guidance, reminding us of fairness, kindness, and justice principles.

It encourages us to respect the possessions, relationships, and accomplishments of others, fostering a sense of integrity and ethical behavior.

Childhood emotional trauma can contribute to the development of envy, jealousy, and covetousness through its impact on an individual's emotional well-being, self-perception, and relational dynamics. Here are several ways in which childhood emotional trauma can lead to these negative inclinations:

- Insecurity and Low Self-Esteem:

Childhood emotional trauma, such as neglect, abuse, or abandonment (which can be physical, emotional, or spiritual), can undermine a child's sense of security and self-worth. This can result in deep-seated feelings of inadequacy and low self-esteem, leading individuals to compare themselves unfavorably with others and covet what they perceive as lacking within themselves.

- Fear of Loss and Scarcity Mindset:

Traumatic experiences in childhood can instill a fear of loss and a scarcity mindset, where individuals feel a need to acquire what they believe is missing in their lives. This fear of scarcity can drive envy and covetousness as individuals seek to compensate for perceived deficiencies caused by past trauma.

Unconditional love operates from a mindset of abundance, believing there is enough love, happiness, and success to go around. In contrast, envy and jealousy are rooted in a scarcity mindset, where individuals think they must compete for limited resources and that someone else's gain is their loss.

- Disrupted Attachment and Trust Issues:

Childhood emotional trauma can disrupt a child's ability to form secure attachments and trust others.

As a result, individuals may struggle with jealousy in relationships and covet the stability and connection that others seem to have due to the lack of secure attachment experienced in childhood. Unconditional love promotes supportive and nurturing behavior, seeking to uplift and empower others.

Envy and jealousy, on the other hand, can lead to destructive and undermining behavior, such as gossip, betrayal, or self-sabotage, as individuals attempt to diminish others to elevate themselves.

Unconditional love builds trust and honesty in relationships, creating an environment of security and openness. Envy and jealousy can erode trust and lead to suspicion, as individuals may become overly protective or doubtful of others' intentions.

- Unresolved Grief and Anger:

Trauma in childhood often leaves individuals with unresolved grief, anger, and other negative emotions.

These unresolved emotions can manifest as jealousy and envy, especially when individuals witness others having what they were denied, leading to bitterness and resentment.

- External Validation and Approval:

Childhood trauma can lead individuals to seek external validation and approval, often comparing themselves to others and coveting the attention, recognition, or love that others appear to receive (this is so evident in our age of social media).

This can result in envy towards those who seem to have the validation and approval they desire. Some go to great detrimental lengths to achieve external validation and acceptance, which is prominent and permeates a vast proportion of today's society.

- Distorted Perceptions and Beliefs:
- Childhood emotional trauma can distort an individual's perceptions and beliefs about themselves, others, and the world.

This distortion can lead to a skewed understanding of success, happiness, and fulfillment, causing individuals to covet what they believe will bring them a sense of security and happiness based on these distorted beliefs.

- Coping Mechanisms and Maladaptive Behaviors:

In response to childhood trauma, individuals may develop maladaptive coping mechanisms, such as jealousy and covetousness, as a means of exerting control or seeking comfort. These behaviors may have been adaptive in the past but can become entrenched and harmful in the long run.

- Reduced Empathy and Emotional Regulation:

Childhood emotional trauma can impact empathy development and emotional regulation, leading to difficulties in understanding and managing emotions. Such challenges can contribute to envy and jealousy as individuals struggle to relate with others and healthily control their feelings.

Unconditional love provides emotional freedom by releasing individuals from the burden of comparison and competition, allowing them to experience deeper connections and fulfillment. Envy and jealousy, on the other hand, lead to emotional turmoil, causing distress, anxiety, and discontent.

The Holy Spirit plays a significant role in helping us overcome envy and jealousy, promoting qualities of love, compassion, and spiritual transformation.

Here are several ways in which the Holy Spirit can assist believers in addressing these negative inclinations:

- Guidance and Wisdom: The Holy Spirit provides guidance and wisdom to us, helping us discern our thoughts, emotions, and actions. In the context of envy and jealousy, the Holy Spirit can illuminate the harmful nature of these emotions and guide us toward a path of love, contentment, and empathy. **Romans 8:9, John 16:1.**

- Transformation of the Heart: the Holy Spirit works within the hearts of believers, transforming us and producing spiritual fruit, including love, joy, peace, and self-control. Through this transformative work, the Holy Spirit can help us cultivate gratitude, compassion, and selflessness, countering envy and jealousy's harmful effects. **Galatians 5:22-23.**

- Empowerment to Love Unconditionally: The Holy Spirit empowers us to love unconditionally, mirroring the divine love demonstrated in the life and teachings of Jesus Christ.

- This empowerment enables us to embrace others with selfless and sacrificial love, freeing us from envy and jealousy. **Romans 5:5, 1 John 4:7-8**

- Healing and Emotional Restoration: God's Holy Spirit is the source of healing and emotional restoration, providing comfort, peace, and inner strength. In the context of envy and jealousy, the Holy Spirit works in our lives, healing emotional wounds, fostering forgiveness, and promoting emotional well-being.

- **Romans 12:2, Ephesians 4:23-24, Philippians 4:8.**

- Conviction and Repentance: The Holy Spirit convicts us of sin, leading us to repentance (turning away from doing wrong) and transformation. In the context of envy and jealousy, the Holy Spirit can bring awareness of these negative emotions, leading us to acknowledge the impact, seek forgiveness, and embark on a journey of personal growth and change. **John 16:8, 1 John 1:9**.

Reflection:

It is essential to recognize that while envy can contribute to wrongful behavior, we all can address and overcome these negative tendencies. By acknowledging the potential impact of envy on our behavior and actively working to manage and lessen these feelings, we can make constructive choices that align with our values and principles. Unconditional love is the opposite of envy and jealousy due to its inherent nature of acceptance, compassion, and abundance.

These biblical principles can serve as a guide for navigating the temptation to envy those who engage in wrongful behavior.

God's unconditional love can transform our hearts and minds, leading us to embrace a perspective centered on love, grace, and forgiveness. This transformation counters the destructive tendencies of envy, jealousy, and covetousness. It fosters a spirit of generosity and goodwill towards others. When we embrace and internalize God's unconditional love, it becomes our guiding light, shaping our attitudes, behaviors, and relationships. Remember that overcoming envy is a process, and seeking support is okay. By actively engaging in these steps and being patient, you can gradually work toward avoiding envious feelings toward those who do wrong.

Envy often stems from a lack of contentment and gratitude. Take a moment to reflect on any areas where envy may exist.

Confess these feelings to God and ask Him to help you cultivate a spirit of gratitude.

Prayer:

Heavenly Father, forgive me for the times when I have allowed envy to overshadow gratitude in my heart. Help me focus on what You have provided rather than comparing myself to others. Teach me how precious I am, of my value and worth in You. Teach me that I am lovable, so much so that You sent Your only Son, Jesus Christ, to die as a ransom for my life. Teach me that I am enough, so I never have to compare myself with another. Fill me with a spirit of contentment and gratitude so that I may truly love others without envy. Help me be sensitive and obedient to Your Holy Spirit so I will cooperate with You to transform my life and produce the fruit of Your Spirit in me.

In Jesus' Name, Amen.

187

Reflection/Note-taking

_____

_____

_____

_____

_____

_____

Reflection/Note-taking

_____

_____

_____

_____

_____

Day 23

Love is Not Proud

1 Corinthians 13:4: "Love Does Not Boast, brag, and is not proud and arrogant."

Devotional:

Pride and self-centeredness will hinder our ability to love unconditionally. My pastor at Remnant Ministries (here in Las Vegas, NV) recently taught about the parable in Luke **14:10-14** that Jesus used to teach about humility. I know this can resonate with many as it did with me. When invited to a function, do not look for the most prominent seat in the venue (so you can feel important) because the host can ask you to move to seat someone else they consider more important. Then, you will be embarrassed to get up and move to a less notable seat. Instead, when invited, go and sit down at the last place so that when the host comes, he will be the one to seat you higher.

You will be honored in the presence of all at the table with you (paraphrased).

This humility can speak to every area of our lives, not only in the church but professionally and personally. It is a lesson for us to not self-promote (for prideful purposes) but allow God to be the one to promote us. Being prideful and arrogant is all about selfishness; love is not selfish. **Verse 11 says**, "For everyone who exalts himself will be humbled (before others), and he who **habitually** humbles himself (keeps a realistic self-view) will be exalted." Jesus went on to say in **verses 13-14** that when you are having a fancy party, do not look to invite only the prominent people, but invite the disabled, the blind, and the lame (those who cannot promote you in a selfish quest for worldly success). You will be blessed because they cannot repay you. Open your heart honestly and ask the Lord to address any areas of pride and arrogance. Pride will always hinder our ability to love unconditionally.

1 Corinthians 13:4 states that love "is not proud, is not arrogant, is not boastful." It speaks to the humility that underlies genuine love.

191

Let us look at these three traits:

Priderefers to an **inflated** sense of self-importance or superiority. Pride can cause us to look down on others and prioritize our needs or opinions above all else. Pride is considered a form of self-centeredness or egotism that can blind a person to their flaws, inhibit their growth, and cause harm to themselves and others. It can lead to a false sense of self-importance and superiority, causing us to be unteachable and resistant to correction or guidance. It can also lead to conflict, as proud individuals may struggle to reconcile or forgive, being more concerned with their status or being correct rather than seeking harmony or showing compassion.

Arrogance: This is characterized by an overbearing attitude based on an **exaggerated** sense of one's abilities or worth. Arrogance can lead to a lack of compassion and empathy, as one may dismiss the values and feelings of others.

Boastfulness: shows **excessive** pride and self-satisfaction in one's achievements, possessions, or abilities. This trait often involves speaking of oneself without regard for others' feelings or contributions.

Let us examine the effects of some of these traits on individuals, families, and society:

Individuals:

Individuals who are proud, arrogant, or boastful struggle with interpersonal relationships. They may isolate themselves or attract conflict, as others perceive them as unapproachable or disrespectful.

I have struggled in this area (and still have times when I must reflect on these teachings when I am drawn back into a prideful state) as I was determined not to lose an argument because of the "need" to be correct. It has damaged relationships both in my personal and professional life.

Now I know that the "need" to be right was all about how I felt about myself (low self-worth) and the need to prove that I was "good enough." Whatever I must prove to anyone is what I do not believe I have in myself. I had called that phase of my life "standing up for myself, being independent, etc." But my pride and arrogance only brought separation and division. Love unifies us, and pride divides us. Humility can lead to personal growth, spiritual development, and positive relationships. It often results in increased resilience, as humble individuals are more likely to learn from their mistakes and failures.

Families:

In a family setting, these behaviors can create tension and undermine trust. When one family member consistently displays arrogance or boastfulness, it can stifle communication and create a competitive rather than a supportive environment.

I have seen this in my own and other families where one spouse is so prideful that it disintegrates communication within the family unit, which can cause a complete collapse and contribute to divorce. I have seen the damaging effects of pride among siblings, cousins, in-laws, and all dynamics of familial relationships.

For example, you may be too proud to apologize or hear another's different opinion. Look within yourself, and admit that you may need help with emotional healing. Some have said that the number one reason for divorces is finances. I want to counteract that and say that it is pride. We have allowed pride to demolish relationships in so many areas.

When family members practice humility, it can lead to greater understanding and better communication, compassion, conflict reduction, and promoting an environment of mutual respect, acceptance, and support.

Debra Enile Armand

Society:

On a societal level, when these negative traits become widespread, they can lead to social layers and a lack of social bonding. Communities thrive on mutual respect and cooperation, so the prevalence of pride, arrogance, and boastfulness can undermine these foundational elements. A society that values humility can experience enhanced cooperation, reduced aggression, and increased kindness. Humble leadership can inspire trust and encourage collective problem-solving. We live in a world today where there are wars and rumors of wars because world leaders are unable or unwilling to humble themselves to live and coexist with other humankind.

We are prideful because we lack and reject God's unconditional love, which is the cure for ALL human ailments. It starts within the human spirit, and we have seen the effects of who we are in our world when our spirits are separated from God. It may sound simplistic, but it is profoundly true.

In contrast to human love, God's love is unconditional, selfless, and all-encompassing. This divine love is pure and given freely without expecting anything in return. It is not based on merit, status, or behavior; it is a gift available to all beings without discrimination. God's love is a guiding and transformative force that encourages personal growth, community, humility, and compassionate action. Embracing His love means to act selflessly, to serve others, and to value the well-being of others as much as your own.

Let us summarize the comparison between pride and God's love, which can be detailed in several aspects:

- Orientation of Focus:

Pride: Inwardly focused on the self, personal achievements, and status. *God's Love*: Outwardly focused on others and their well-being and a relationship that originates, continually resides, and survives in God.

- Effects on Relationships:

Pride: Can cause division, strife, and isolation; damages connections with others.

God's Love: Fosters unity, reconciliation, and community; strengthens bonds with others.

- Perception of Self and Others:

Pride: Often inflates self-perception and diminishes others; sees worth hierarchically.

God's Love: Recognizes equality of all beings; sees intrinsic worth in everyone.

- Approach to Mistakes and Learning:

Pride: Resist acknowledgment of wrongdoings or faults; reluctance to learn from others.

God's Love: Encourages humility, repentance, growth, and a willingness to learn.

- Response to Success and Failure:

Pride: Success may lead to arrogance; failure may be met with denial or blame.

God's Love: Success is shared and used to uplift others; failure is accepted with grace and as an opportunity to improve.

- Sustainability and Legacy:

Pride: Pride is often unsustainable because it is built on fragile self-concepts and comparison; its legacy may be tinged with conflict.

God's Love: Creates a lasting, positive impact; legacy of kindness, compassion, and community.

The Bible offers the following approaches to counteract pride, arrogance, and boastfulness:

- Humility: **Philippians 2:3** advises, "Do nothing out of selfish ambition or vain conceit. Rather, in humility, value others above yourselves." Humility is recognizing and valuing others and acknowledging their worth and contributions.

- Service: Serving others, as demonstrated by Jesus washing His disciples' feet (**John 13:1-17**), is a powerful antidote to pride and arrogance. It involves putting others' needs before one's own.

- Compassion and Empathy: **Colossians 3:12-13** encourages believers to "Clothe yourselves with compassion, kindness, humility, gentleness, and patience."

By developing empathy, one can better understand and connect with the experiences of others.

- Accountability: Having a community that holds one accountable, as suggested in **Hebrews 10:24-25**, can help keep pride at bay and can encourage actions that build up rather than tear down.

- Love as Action: **1 John 3:18** espouses, "Let us not love with words or speech but with actions and in truth." Love requires active engagement and sincere actions, not just mere declarations.

By applying these biblical principles, an individual can uproot the tendency toward pride, arrogance, and boastfulness and replace them with the humility and selfless love that exemplify the Christian faith. In the Bible, humility is often associated with wisdom, honor, and spiritual insight.

Some more Biblical References and Examples

- **Philippians 2:3-11**: This passage encourages believers to emulate the humility of Christ, who, despite being divine, took on the nature of a servant and was obedient to death on the cross. Humility is not popular in our world culture. It is counter-culture to what we are taught.

- We are encouraged to look out for ourselves and make self # 1, regardless of how it negatively affects others. **Verse 3** says to do nothing from selfishness or empty conceit (through factional motives or strife), but with (an attitude of) humility (being neither arrogant nor self-righteous), regard others as more important than ourselves.

Verse 4 reiterates, do not merely look out for your interests, but also for the interests of others. Continue to study this passage to see how God Himself, through Jesus Christ, laid aside His Divinity to take on the form of a human being, putting our interests (the salvation of our souls, reconciliation to Him that was lost through sin) above His own. This is love.

- **Proverbs 22:4**: "By humility and the fear of the LORD are riches, honor, and life." This passage links humility (an attitude of selflessness and a recognition of our limitations and dependence on God) with reverence for God (deep respect for His power, majesty, and authority) and demonstrates its resultant blessings.

The riches here do not necessarily solely refer to material wealth. Riches can also be spiritual abundances, such as wisdom, inner peace (which we desperately seek), and a fulfilling life based on our communion with a God who desperately loves us.

I have met people who have exemplified this humility and shone brighter than kings and queens of this earth. Mother Teresa of Kolkata, India, tirelessly worked to serve people experiencing poverty and was honored with a Nobel Peace Prize in 1979. Mahatma Gandhi was known for his humble and non-violent approach to governmental and societal changes and was honored nationally and globally. Nelson Mandela showed humility and a forgiving attitude as he emerged from a 27-year imprisonment without bitterness. He led South Africa through reconciliation and away from racial segregation. He, too, received a Nobel Peace Prize in 1993. Dr Martin Luther King Jr. exemplified humility in his unwavering commitment to racial justice and equality. He also was honored with a Nobel Peace Prize in 1964.

Many more individuals who did not serve others for recognition, honor of man, or to seek worldly riches still exist.

We may never receive a Nobel Peace Prize here on this earth, but God will reward us with His Prize of honor. Humility flows from a heart of unconditional love.

Additional scriptures regarding humility:

- **Matthew 18:4**: "Whosoever therefore shall humble himself as this little child, the same is greatest in the kingdom of heaven." Here, Jesus uses a child as an example to teach the importance of humility.

- **James 4:6**: "But he gives more grace. Therefore, it says, God opposes the proud but gives grace to the humble." This verse indicates that God favors the humble and provides them with grace.

- **1 Peter 5:5-6**: "Likewise, you who are younger, be subject to the elders. Clothe yourselves, all of you, with humility toward one another, for God opposes the proud but gives grace to the humble. Humble yourselves, therefore, under the mighty hand of God so that at the proper time he may exalt you."

Reflection:

Practical Applications in Everyday Life

Listen More**: Reserve judgment and allow others to speak, genuinely listening to their viewpoints with an open mind. This can be learned if it is difficult.

- Acknowledge Limitations**: Be willing to admit when you do not know something or have made a mistake and be open to learning from others. Understand that not knowing something has nothing to do with your worth.

- Seek Feedback**: Invite and accept constructive criticism with a view to self-improvement rather than defensiveness.

- Show Appreciation**: Regularly express gratitude for what you have and for the contributions of others.

- Serve Others**: Look for opportunities to help others without seeking recognition or reward.

- Practice Mindfulness**:

- Exercise self-awareness and consider the impact of your words and actions on others. This is a significant step toward spiritual and emotional healing and maturity.

- Self-Reflect**: Spend time in personal reflection or prayer, considering ways to align your life with the values of humility.

In short, the Lord's warning against pride and the commandment to embrace love reflects a call to transform from self-centered beings into individuals who can live life fully and abundantly while contributing positively to the world around us, recognizing the interconnectedness of all life. This transformation is essential for developing our character and the very health of our souls. Take time to reflect on areas where pride, arrogance, and boasting may be present. Ask God to reveal these areas and pray for a humble heart. Pride builds walls, destroys relationships, and makes it difficult to love unconditionally.

Spend time today reflecting on your attitude toward pride and asking God to help you embrace humility, fostering connections with others.

Prayer:

Lord, I come to You with an open heart. Please show me my heart and give me Your grace to lay aside any pride and boasting within me. Please remove any trace of pride from my heart and teach me the beauty of humility. Help me value and honor others, yield to Your will, and extend love without being hindered by pride. Help me recognize that all good things come from You and boast only in Your love and grace. I know I cannot do this without Your love continually abiding in my heart. I understand and believe You want what is best for me and those around me. Fill me with humility to reflect Your love to others without seeking recognition or praise.

In Jesus' Name, Amen.

Reflection/Note-taking

Reflection/Note-taking

_____

_____

_____

_____

_____

Day 24

Love is not Rude

1 Corinthians 13:5: "Love is Not Rude (It does not dishonor others)."

Devotional:

The previous chapter ties into this: being rude to others results from a prideful heart. As we reflected earlier, pridefulness gives us an exaggerated perception of a false sense of inflated self-esteem regarding our values and accomplishments as we compare ourselves to others. This can lead us to have a dismissive or superior attitude toward others, making us feel that, in some way, we are better than them, which can easily translate into disrespectful behaviors toward them.

Being disrespectful involves acting impolitely or inconsiderately toward others' feelings and well-being. It is an external expression of the internal attitude of pride.

Both pride and disrespect result from a lack of unconditional love in our hearts.

Pride disrupts love's humble and selfless nature, while disrespect directly conflicts with love's kindness and patience. Together, they illustrate how they both originate from self-centeredness and a lack of regard for others. Remember that true love is humble, patient, kind, and selfless. I will reiterate here that disrespect or rudeness is the outward behavior that results from an inner attitude of pride.

Reflection:

In a world where rudeness is prevalent, we must strive to extend grace and kindness. Review some of the practical applications in the previous chapter, commit to memory the scriptures on humility, compassion, serving others, gratitude, and your sense of self-worth that originates in your identity in Christ, to name a few.

The Word of God is your shield, spiritually, mentally, and emotionally, from the onslaught of attacks you will receive from the enemy of your soul.

211

The Word of God is your spiritual sword to demolish worldly lies that want to or have taken root and strongholds in your life that have kept you imprisoned in your mind and spirit. Christ has demolished all those weapons that have formed against you and have given you freedom in Him. You are no longer obligated to walk in your old sinful nature but can now be free to live and love like Christ.

Take a moment to examine your words and actions, asking God to help you be intentional in being respectful toward others.

Prayer:

Loving Father, I humbly come before You, recognizing when I have been rude or disrespectful to others. I ask for Your forgiveness and pray that You transform my heart.

Help me be mindful of how my words and actions impact others so that I may exemplify Your love through kindness and respect.

In Jesus' Name, Amen.

Day 25

Love is Not Self-Seeking

1 Corinthians 13:5: Love is not rude; it is not self-seeking (conditional or transactional).

Devotional:

We have discussed the definition of true unconditional love versus conditional or transactional love extensively. The world is beginning to realize that conditional love lacks what our soul needs and it is not sustainable. This book is about **unlearning the façade** and **embracing the truth** to change the trajectory of our lives and relationships. It is countercultural to society's definition.

Reflect on your motivations and desires today. Think of how many times we have prayed for something, and it seems God did not answer that prayer. There can be many reasons for that. It is possible that what we asked for was not good or God's will for us.

213

He sees the beginning from the end, and if we believe He will hold no good thing from us because every good and perfect gift comes from above, then we must be honest with ourselves to examine the motives behind what we are praying for. His Word teaches us that we have not because we ask not, and when we ask, we do so with the wrong motives.

Reflection:

Reflect on today's scripture and remind yourself that love is not self-seeking. Are you more focused on what you can gain for yourself or on how you can love and serve others? Take a moment to examine your heart and ask God to align your intentions with His selfless love.

Prayer:

Heavenly Father, forgive me for the times when I have been self-centered and focused on my desires. Help me to shift my focus toward selfless love, just as You demonstrated Your love for us through Jesus.

Teach me to seek the well-being and happiness of others, putting their needs before mine.

In Jesus' Name, Amen.

Day 26

Love is Not Easily Angered

1 Corinthians 13:5 Love is not provoked (nor overly sensitive and easily angered).

<u>Devotional:</u>

Whether you believe in Christ or not, people are acutely aware that the world has become an angry and volatile place to live. We see it in individuals, families, communities, and nations. People are easily triggered and can explode at the slightest infraction, which can, at times, lead to fatal consequences, thus contributing to an increasing crime rate and world wars. Uncontrolled anger is a familial, corporate, and societal problem that needs to be resolved beyond laws, rules, and regulations. It is an internal problem that must be addressed emotionally and spiritually.

The Bible teaches us many things about love, and one of the essential truths is found in **1 Corinthians 13:5,** which says that love is not easily angered.

Uncontrolled anger is a destructive force that can significantly impact individuals, families, society, and the world. It is a **lack of self-control**, a failure to manage and regulate emotions. When we allow ourselves to be easily angered, we allow our emotions to overcome reason and wisdom, leading to irrational behavior and unproductive outcomes. One of the effects of uncontrolled anger on an individual is that it can lead to a breakdown in personal and professional relationships. When we allow our anger to control us, we often say and do things we regret later. This can lead to fractured relationships, isolation, and an overall sense of unfulfillment.

Furthermore, uncontrolled anger can lead to stress, anxiety, and even physical health problems, such as high blood pressure, heart disease, and other health issues.

Uncontrolled anger also can have a significant impact on families, as it can lead to a cycle of abuse and dysfunction.

Children who witness uncontrolled anger in their parents are likely to internalize this behavior and perpetuate the cycle of anger and violence. This violent cycle has the potential to destroy families and create a generational pattern of dysfunction.

On a larger scale, uncontrolled anger can significantly impact society, leading to conflict, violence, terrorism, and wars. History is littered with examples of how uncontrolled outrage has led to destructive outcomes. From domestic violence to international strife, unchecked anger can tear apart the fabric of society and lead to untold suffering.

In the Bible, we see numerous examples of the destructive power of uncontrolled anger.

In **Genesis 4:1-16,** we read about how Cain's uncontrolled outrage led him to murder his brother Abel. **Proverbs 15:18** says, "A hot-tempered person stirs up conflict, but the one who is patient calms a quarrel."

Similarly, in **Ephesians 4:31-32**, we are encouraged to "Get rid of all bitterness, rage and anger, brawling and slander, along with every form of malice. Be kind and compassionate to one another, forgiving each other, just as in Christ God forgave you."

So, what is the solution to uncontrolled anger? The Bible guides us on managing our emotions and cultivating **love instead of anger. Galatians 5:22-23** mentions that a fruit of the Spirit is self-control. Through prayer, seeking God's guidance, and relying on the Holy Spirit, we can develop the self-control necessary to manage our emotions and respond to situations with love instead of anger.

Additionally, practicing forgiveness and seeking reconciliation can help heal relationships damaged by uncontrolled anger.

1 Corinthians 13:5 teaches us that love is not easily angered.

Through the guidance of biblical teachings that will help us to know and experience God in a personal way, we can learn to cultivate love and self-control (which are some of the beautiful fruit that God's Holy Spirit will bear in our lives as we follow Him) and overcome uncontrolled anger.

The Bible offers us wisdom and guidance to replace anger with love and to build healthy, fulfilling relationships that honor God. I reiterate that healthy relationships can only be accomplished by the power of God's Holy Spirit living and moving through us, which will mature and sustain unconditional love in our lives.

1 Corinthians 13:5 is a powerful verse that states, "It (love) does not dishonor others, it is not self-seeking, it is not easily angered, it keeps no record of wrongs."

Love is significant in relationships, as it emphasizes the importance of patience, understanding, and forgiveness and is not easily angered.

Many people struggle with uncontrolled and suppressed anger, a common issue. It occurs when individuals unable to manage their emotions react impulsively with rage, hostility, or violence, leading to harmful behaviors and negative consequences for the person experiencing the anger, as well as those around them. Anger can have a variety of root causes, including past trauma, stress, unmet needs or expectations, or underlying mental health issues.

Uncontrolled anger can destroy all aspects of an individual's life when left unaddressed. The effects can be devastating on an individual level. It can lead to physical and emotional health issues, such as high blood pressure, heart disease, anxiety, depression, and substance abuse.

Additionally, uncontrolled anger can damage relationships with loved ones, as it can lead to verbal, emotional, or physical abuse. It can also hinder an individual's ability to communicate effectively and make rational decisions.

Furthermore, anger can hinder personal and professional success, leading to difficulties in managing stress and conflict. The impact of this extends beyond the individual to families, society, and the world at large. In terms of families, anger can create a hostile or toxic environment, leading to damage in relationships and harm to children who witness or experience the anger. It can contribute to the breakdown of marriages, divorce, and fractured family dynamics. Uncontrolled anger can manifest in crime, violence, and social unrest which can result in a culture of aggression, conflict, and division, creating barriers to empathy and understanding.

On a global scale, uncontrolled anger can fuel conflict and war, leading to widespread suffering and destruction. The Bible provides several examples of the destructive nature of anger. In the New Testament, Jesus speaks against uncontrolled anger, warning that it can lead to judgment and punishment (**Matthew 5:22**). The Bible offers solutions for managing anger and promoting love. One of the fundamental teachings is the importance of self-control and patience (manifestations of unconditional love).

In **Galatians 5:22-23**, the fruit of the spirit includes love, patience, and self-control, which can help individuals manage their emotions and respond to conflict more constructively.

Additionally, the Bible emphasizes the value of forgiveness and reconciliation. In **Ephesians 4:26-27**, we are admonished not to let the sun go down on our anger and not to give the devil a foothold, highlighting the need for timely resolution and peace.

Finally, the Bible encourages the practice of empathy and understanding toward others, as in **Colossians 3:13,** which urges us to bear with each other and forgive one another if any of us has a grievance against someone.

Some scriptures on anger:

- Moses and the rock (**Numbers 20:8-12**) - Moses' uncontrolled anger led him to disobey God's command and strike the rock angrily, resulting in him being forbidden from entering the promised land.

- **Proverbs 29:22** - "An angry person stirs up conflict, and a hot-tempered person commits many sins."

- **Ephesians 4:26-27** - "In your anger do not sin: Do not let the sun go down while you are still angry, and do not give the devil a foothold."

- **Proverbs 15:1** - "A gentle answer turns away wrath, but a harsh word stirs up anger."

- **James 1:19-20** - "My dear brothers and sisters, take note of this: Everyone should be quick to listen, slow to speak and slow to become angry, because human anger does not produce the righteousness that God desires."

- **Ephesians 4:31-32** - "Get rid of all bitterness, rage and anger, brawling and slander, along with every form of malice. Be kind and compassionate to one another, forgiving each other, just as in Christ God forgave you."

- **Proverbs 29:11** states, "Fools give full vent to their rage, but the wise bring calm in the end."

- **Proverbs 14:17** states, "A quick-tempered person does foolish things, and the one who devises evil schemes is hated."

- This verse highlights the negative impact of uncontrolled anger on a person's behavior and relationships. It suggests that unchecked anger can lead to foolish, harmful actions and strained relationships.

1 Corinthians 13:5 states that love is not easily angered. This passage highlights the importance of patience, forgiveness, and self-control in relationships.

This contrasts with prevalent attitudes towards anger in modern society, where anger is often seen as a natural and justifiable response to various situations. Additionally, there is a pervasive emphasis on expressing and acting on one's anger, often without considering the potential consequences for others.

Love, not easily angered, encourages individuals to navigate conflicts and challenges with a calm and understanding demeanor, which may differ from the societal norm of escalating or acting out in anger.

This contrast highlights the countercultural nature of biblical concepts. It underscores the value of approaching relationships, focusing on patience, empathy, and self-restraint.

In contrast, contemporary culture often normalizes and glorifies anger to express empowerment or assert dominance.

Social media, entertainment, and political discourse frequently validate and promote the expression of anger as a legitimate response to various issues and conflicts. This can normalize hostile and aggressive behaviors, creating a cycle of negativity and conflict. In many cases, anger is glamorized in popular culture and used as a tool for conflict resolution or personal empowerment.

The normalization of anger in society can lead to destructive behaviors and strained relationships, as it can contribute to a cycle of retaliation and hostility. Popular media often depicts anger and aggression as powerful and satisfying emotions, with characters lashing out in moments of frustration or stress.

Debra Enile Armand

This can create a glamorized view of anger, portraying it as a justified and heroic response to adversity. The impact of these depictions on societal attitudes toward anger can be significant.

By perpetuating the idea that anger and aggression are normal and acceptable responses to conflict or distress, popular media can potentially normalize and even encourage aggressive behavior in real life. This can lead to an increase in aggressive and confrontational attitudes, contributing to a culture that condones violent and destructive behavior.

The portrayal of anger and aggression in popular media can perpetuate harmful stereotypes and reinforce toxic masculinity, leading to a glorification of aggressive behavior, especially among young, impressionable audiences. Just take an in-depth look at some of social media's influences behind school shooters.

This conflicts with the biblical understanding of love's patience, as the Bible teaches that love is patient and kind and that anger should be managed and controlled.

The Bible also emphasizes the importance of forgiveness and understanding, even in the face of provocation or wrongdoing. We must be mindful of these conflicting messages and strive to embody the virtues of love, patience, and forgiveness as the Bible teaches. **1 Corinthians 13:5** reminds us of the destructive nature of uncontrolled anger and the importance of cultivating love and patience in our relationships.

Reflection:

We are cautioned to slow down and think before reacting in anger. As one of my mentors, Pete Uglow, would say, "Practice the Pause." **James 1:19-20** says, "My dear brothers and sisters, take note of this:

Everyone should be quick to listen, slow to speak and slow to become angry, because human anger does not produce the righteousness that God desires."

Practical steps that we can take to overcome anger include:

1. Take a moment to pause and breathe before reacting impulsively in anger.

2. Practice forgiveness and releasing past hurts and resentments. Let go of grudges. Learn about God's character, that He is a just Judge, and leave vengeance in His Hands.

3. Seek wise counsel and guidance from trusted individuals. Seek spiritual support through prayer and meditation on God's Word as you seek God's guidance in managing anger.

4. Learn to communicate assertively and effectively, with love, to express your feelings and needs.

5. Engage in self-care activities such as exercise, relaxation techniques, and mindfulness to manage stress and emotions.

6. Practice empathy and understanding. The Bible teaches us to put ourselves in others' shoes and understand their perspective before reacting angrily. This can help us respond with compassion and forgiveness instead of anger.

7. Practice self-control: The Bible encourages us to practice self-control and manage our emotions, especially when angry. Practice yielding your will to God's will as you abide in Him and allow His Holy Spirit to develop His fruit of self-control in you. By controlling our feelings, we can respond to situations with clear thinking and a calm demeanor.

8. Seek reconciliation: The Bible emphasizes the importance of seeking reconciliation with others, even if it means putting aside our pride. This can involve apologizing, seeking forgiveness, and repairing the relationship, if possible.

9. Pray for strength and guidance: The Bible encourages us to seek strength and guidance from God in times of anger and conflict.

By turning to prayer, we can find peace and clarity in overcoming our anger and promoting forgiveness and reconciliation.

10. Renew your mind by finding and committing to memory the Truth of God's Word to develop a deep, abiding personal relationship with Him and His unconditional love for you and others.

I cannot emphasize enough that our human strength or power cannot accomplish this consistently and for the long term. Still, it can and will be done by God's Spirit in us (**Zechariah 4:6**).

We all need the power of God's Holy Spirit living in us to bring about the fruit of self-control and love in our lives as we yield to His teachings and guidance.

God gives us a choice to either be controlled by our human nature without Christ (sinful, carnal nature that will lead to self-destruction, **Galatians 5:1-21**) or give our lives over to Him and be controlled by His Holy Spirit, yielding the fruit of love (unselfish concern for others), joy (inner) peace, patience, (how we act while we wait), kindness, goodness, faithfulness, gentleness, self-control **Galatians 5:22-23**.

Read, study, and spend some time in the entire chapter of **Galatians 5.**

In conclusion, **1 Corinthians 13:5** reminds us that love is not easily angered, highlighting the importance of managing emotions and promoting understanding and forgiveness in relationships.

Uncontrolled anger can have devastating effects on individuals, families, society, and the world, leading to physical and emotional harm, conflict, and suffering.

The Bible provides:

- Guidance in managing anger.
- Emphasis on the importance of self-control.
- Forgiveness.
- Empathy in promoting love and peace.

God's unconditional love resolves our inner turmoil, family dysfunctions, and societal problems. Consider situations that tend to trigger your anger or frustration.

Prayer:

Gracious Lord, I confess that I struggle with anger at times. Teach me Your love in a personal way. Love and heal me so I can be transformed into Your image and likeness, so Your Holy Spirit can bear fruit in me that I can extend to others. Help me to see myself and others through Your eyes. Grant me the wisdom and strength to respond to frustrating situations with love and understanding.

Your love is patient, so help me to be controlled by Your Spirit. Help me to control my emotions and let Your peace reign in my heart so that I may be a vessel of Your love to those around me.

In Jesus' Name, Amen.

Reflection/Note-taking

_____

_____

_____

_____

_____

Debra Enile Armand

Reflection/Note-taking

_____

_____

_____

_____

_____

_____

Day 27

Love Keeps No Record of Wrongs

1 Corinthians 13:5: "It does not dishonor others, it is not self-seeking, it is not easily angered, it keeps no record of wrongs."

Devotional:

1 Corinthians 13:5 is a powerful verse that highlights the nature of love. It states, "It keeps no record of wrongs." This means that love does not hold on to past mistakes or grievances but instead chooses to forgive and move forward. In our daily lives, we are called to release past hurts and offenses and to extend grace and forgiveness to those who have wronged us. This aligns with other biblical teachings on forgiveness, such as **Colossians 3:13**, which says, "Bear with each other and forgive one another if any of you has a grievance against someone. Forgive as the Lord forgave you."

Psalm 103:12 has become one of my transformative scriptures that has come alive in my daily life regarding being forgiven and forgiving others.

Debra Enile Armand

It says, "As far as the east is from the west (the two never meet), so far has He (God in Christ) removed our transgressions from us." God has and continues to forgive me every moment of every day. He promises us in **Isaiah 43 25**, "I (God), only I, am He who wipes out your transgressions for My (His) own sake and will not remember your sins." What would our lives be like if God recorded all the wrongs we thought and acted out?

The effects of holding grudges are detrimental to individuals, families, society, and the world. Holding on to past wrongs can lead to bitterness, resentment, and broken relationships. Also, it can create a toxic environment in families and communities, hindering reconciliation and unity. Moreover, societal and global conflicts often stem from long-standing grudges and unforgiveness.

Look around at our world today and the nations at war with each other in the Middle East, Europe, and Asian countries.

As Christians, we are peacemakers and should demonstrate love and forgiveness in all aspects of our lives (**Matthew 5:9**). By choosing to let go of past wrongs and to forgive others, we can promote healing, restoration, and unity in our personal lives, families, communities, and the world.

According to biblical teachings, holding grudges and keeping records of wrongdoing in our relationships can lead to several potential consequences:

1. Bitterness and resentment: Tracking past wrongs can lead to anger and ill will, poisoning relationships and hindering forgiveness and reconciliation.

2. Strained relationships: Holding onto grudges can create friction and tension in relationships, causing distance and division between individuals.

3. Hindered prayer life: The Bible teaches that unforgiveness can hinder our prayers (**Mark 11:25),** preventing us from experiencing the fullness of God's blessings and favor.

4. Spiritual bondage: Refusing to forgive and letting go of grudges can lead to spiritual bondage and a lack of freedom in relationships and personal life.

5. Judgment from God: The Bible warns that if we do not forgive others, God will not forgive us (**Matthew 6:14-15**), emphasizing the importance of forgiveness in our relationships.

By holding unto grudges and keeping a record of wrongdoing can result in negative spiritual, emotional, and relational consequences, hindering our ability to experience peace, joy, and healthy relationships.

The Bible instructs believers to handle conflict resolution within relationships in several ways:

1. Seek reconciliation: In **Matthew 5:23-24**, Jesus instructs believers to reconcile with others before coming to worship.

2. Address issues directly: In **Matthew 18:15-17,** Jesus sets out a process for addressing conflicts within the church, starting with addressing the issue directly with the person involved. This approach of open communication and loving confrontation is encouraged to resolve disputes.

3. Offer forgiveness: The Bible repeatedly emphasizes the importance of forgiveness in resolving conflicts. **Colossians 3:13 teaches** believers to forgive as the Lord forgave them.

4. Show love and kindness: In **Romans 12:17-21**, we are counseled to respond to evil with goodness and love and to live at peace with others as far as it depends on them.

God's Word instructs us to resolve conflicts in our relationships with humility, grace, forgiveness, and a commitment to seeking reconciliation and peace.

Reflection:

This verse for today counsels that love does not keep a record of wrongs, meaning it does not harbor grudges or hold past mistakes against someone. Applying this principle to our daily relationships means choosing to forgive and letting go of the wrongs committed by others rather than holding onto anger or seeking revenge. It encourages us to approach interactions with grace and understanding, allowing room for growth and reconciliation. By embodying this attitude, we can foster healthier, more compassionate relationships with those around us.

Love is a choice, and so is forgiveness. Love is a fruit of the Spirit. Think about any grudges or past hurts that you have been holding onto. Are there any resentments you need to release to embrace love fully?

Take a moment to bring these burdens to the Lord and ask Him to help you forgive and let go of any lingering pain.

Prayer:

Dear Father, I bring to You any resentments and grudges that I have been holding onto. I know now that they have only served to hurt others, myself, and my relationship with You.

I have been unable to truly experience and abide in Your unconditional love because this has been a barrier for Your love to flow in and through me. Please help me to release these burdens, grant me the strength to forgive, and fill my heart with Your love. Teach me to keep no record of wrongs, just as You forgive and forget our sins.

In Jesus' Name, Amen.

Reflection/Note-taking

_____

_____

_____

_____

_____

Debra Enile Armand

Reflection/Note-taking

_____

_____

_____

_____

_____

Day 28

Love Does Not Delight in Evil

1 Corinthian 13:6: "Love does not rejoice at injustice (evil) but rejoices with the truth (when right and truth prevail)."

Devotional:

1 Corinthians 13:6 states, "Love does not delight in evil but rejoices with the truth." This verse is a part of the famous passage known as the "Love Chapter," where the Apostle Paul eloquently describes the characteristics of love. In this verse, Paul emphasizes that true love does not find pleasure in wrongdoing but instead finds joy in honesty and righteousness.

The definition of love not delighting in evil is a call for us to reject and abstain from participating in anything contrary to God's truth and goodness.

It requires a discerning mind and a heart oriented toward righteousness and integrity.

Unconditional love is a commitment to uphold moral values and ethical conduct.

When individuals, families, and society fail to adhere to the principle of not delighting in evil and instead revel in dishonesty, immorality, and wrongdoing, it leads to a host of adverse effects. Individually, delighting in evil can result in a lack of integrity and moral decay. When people take pleasure in evil, they become desensitized to the consequences of their actions and become more inclined to engage in unethical behavior, whether it is lying, cheating, or hurting others for personal gain. This can lead to a breakdown of trust and respect in personal relationships and harm a person's character and reputation.

A toxic and dysfunctional environment will flourish when family members find joy rather than uphold the truth.

Dishonesty, infidelity, and selfishness can erode the foundation of love and trust for a healthy family dynamic.

A lack of love and rejoicing in the truth can result in broken relationships, emotional turmoil, and a lack of cohesion within the family unit.

On a societal level, the consequences of not delighting in evil and rejoicing in the truth are far-reaching. When a society embraces corruption, deceit, and immorality, it can lead to a culture of lawlessness, injustice, and moral decadence. This can manifest in various forms, such as widespread social unrest, crime, and societal inequalities. Additionally, the erosion of truth and goodness can devastate individuals' mental and emotional well-being, leading to hopelessness and disillusionment.

The biblical solution to this issue is to cultivate a heart and mind that seeks after truth, righteousness, and love. The Bible teaches that love and truth are inseparable and that true love always seeks what is good and right.

In **Ephesians 4:15,** the Apostle Paul urges us to speak the truth in love, emphasizing the importance of operating in love while upholding honesty and integrity.

Moreover, the Bible also teaches that the renewal of the mind and the transformation of the heart are essential in aligning oneself with the principles of love and truth. **Romans 12:2** encourages believers not to conform to the pattern of this world but to be transformed by renewing the mind. This transformation occurs through deepening one's relationship with God, studying His Word, and being guided by the Holy Spirit.

1 Corinthians 13:6 underscores the importance of love not delighting in evil and rejoicing in the truth. When individuals, families, and society embrace these principles, they lead to a flourishing and harmonious existence. When the opposite occurs, the adverse effects are pervasive and destructive.

By aligning with the biblical teachings of love
and truth, we can find the strength and guidance to
resist the allure of evil and uphold the principles of
righteousness and integrity in their lives.

1 Corinthians 13:6 states that love "rejoices in
the truth." This verse emphasizes the importance of
truth and honesty in relationships and how love
should be rooted in these principles. However, in
today's society, the lack of truth and honesty has
negatively affected individuals, families, and
everyone around us. Let us explore the definition of
truth, the harmful effects of the absence of truth, and
biblical solutions for addressing this issue.

Definition of Truth

Truth can be defined as the quality or state of
being in accordance with fact or reality.

God's Word is Truth (**John 17:17, Psalm
119:160**). Jesus is the Truth (**John 14:6, John 1:14,
John 1:17**).

Truth is the absence of deceit or falsehood and
the presence of sincerity and honesty. We have an

enemy of the Truth, who is Satan, and his goal is to keep us from the Truth to ensure we suffer the consequences of living in and for his lies (**John 8:44, 2 Corinthians 11:14, Revelation 12:9**). In the context of **1 Corinthians 13:6,** love should not be built on lies or deception.

<u>Harmful Effects on Individuals</u>

The absence of truth in relationships can have detrimental effects on individuals. It can lead to feelings of betrayal, mistrust, and insecurity. When individuals are not truthful, it results in a lack of intimacy and connection in relationships. This has the potential to hurt one's mental and emotional well-being, bringing about stress, anxiety, and depression.

<u>Harmful Effects on Families</u>

The absence of truth can lead to conflicts and communication breakdowns in families. When family members are not honest with each other, it can create a toxic and dysfunctional environment.

Lack of trust and honesty can give rise to strained relationships and resentment within the family unit. This can ultimately lead to the family structure's disintegration and negatively impact its members' overall well-being.

Harmful Effects on Society

On a larger scale, the absence of truth in society can cause widespread distrust and division. When individuals and institutions are not truthful, it can erode the fabric of society and lead to a breakdown in social cohesion. A lack of truth in public communication and media can result in misinformation and manipulation, ultimately leading to societal unrest and instability.

Biblical Solutions

The Bible offers several solutions to the issue of truth. First, it teaches the importance of personal integrity and honesty. **Proverbs 12:22** states, "The Lord detests lying lips, but He delights in people who are trustworthy."

This verse emphasizes the value of truth and the need for individuals to be truthful in their words and actions.

Secondly, the Bible encourages reconciliation and restoration in relationships. In **Matthew 5:23-24**, Jesus teaches, "Therefore, if you are offering your gift at the altar and there remember that your brother or sister has something against you, leave your gift there in front of the altar. First, go and be reconciled to them; then come and offer your gift." This verse highlights the importance of honesty and making amends in relationships, emphasizing the need for truth in resolving conflicts.

Lastly, the Bible teaches the importance of seeking wisdom and discernment. **Proverbs 3:5-6** states, "Trust in the Lord with all your heart and lean not on your own understanding; in all your ways submit to Him, and He will make your paths straight." This verse emphasizes the need for seeking God's wisdom and guidance in all aspects of life, including the pursuit of truth.

1 Corinthians 13:6 emphasizes the importance of truth in relationships and the detrimental effects of its absence. The lack of truth can negatively impact everyone. By embracing these biblical principles, individuals can strive to build relationships and communities rooted in truth and honesty, ultimately leading to greater unity and well-being.

The absence of Truth and celebrating wrongdoing can hurt societal norms and values. When love is absent, people may act selfishly and without consideration for others, leading to a breakdown of empathy and compassion. Such breakdown can lead to a culture of individualism and self-centeredness, where people prioritize their own needs and desires above the well-being of others. It promotes a disregard for ethical behavior and a tolerance for injustice.

When wrongdoing is celebrated, it normalizes unethical behavior and diminishes the importance of moral values and integrity within a society. The repercussions of the absence of Truth and the celebration of delighting in evil can result in a decline in social cohesion, increased conflict and division, and a lack of trust and respect among community members. Additionally, these attitudes can contribute to a culture of corruption, discrimination, and injustice, further eroding society's fabric.

We as individuals and communities are encouraged embrace love and compassion and uphold moral values and ethical behavior to lessen these undesirable impacts. By promoting God's Truth and condemning evil, societies can foster a culture of empathy, cooperation, and justice, leading to a more harmonious and equitable social environment. When society tolerates those who lie and promote evil-doing, unethical behavior results.

On the other hand, a society that strongly condemns evil and wrongdoing and holds individuals accountable for their actions is more likely to foster a culture of ethical behavior and uphold moral values. In such a society, individuals may be more inclined to adhere to moral principles and resist engaging in these behaviors, as they are aware of the consequences and social disapproval that may result.

1. Individual Solution: The Bible encourages us to cultivate love, truth, and righteousness by seeking a personal relationship with God, the Source of these things.

2. Family Solution: Families are encouraged to prioritize love, truth, and righteousness within the home by modeling these values in their relationships. This can involve fostering open and honest communication, showing compassion and forgiveness, and upholding moral and ethical standards in all family life.

3.Societal Solution: The Lord teaches that love, truth, and righteousness should be the foundation of a just and harmonious society. See scriptures such as **Proverbs 14:34, Psalm 33:12, Psalm 72:1-3**.

4.This can be achieved through promoting social justice, advocating for the rights of the marginalized and vulnerable, and working towards the common good of all members of society.

Additionally, individuals must be agents of positive change by actively living out love, truth, and righteousness in their communities and seeking to influence others to do the same.

<u>Reflection:</u>

Examine your reactions to negativity and wrongdoing. Do you find satisfaction in others' misfortune or tend to gossip? Pray for God to transform your heart, enabling you to genuinely care for others and seek their good, even when they falter.

Prayer:

Loving God, forgive me for when I have found delight in others' misfortunes. Transform my heart so that I may genuinely care for and encourage those around me. Give me the ability to love unconditionally, even when faced with wrongdoing, and enable me to be a beacon of Your love and grace. In Jesus' Name, Amen.

As you meditate on these reflections and offer your prayers, may God's love continuously shape your heart, guiding you to demonstrate His love to others in all circumstances. May His love overflow through you, bringing hope, healing, and reconciliation to a broken world.

Reflection/Note-taking

_____

_____

_____

_____

_____

_____

Reflection/Note-taking

_____

_____

_____

_____

_____

Day 29

Love Rejoices in Truth

1 Corinthians 13:6: "It does not rejoice at injustice, but rejoices with the truth [when right and truth prevail]."

Devotional:

Telling the truth and not being afraid to do so is gradually becoming my new reality as I continue this fantastic journey of unlearning love (the world's definition) and embracing unconditional love. As far back as I remember as a child, telling the truth brought more punishment than reward. One example was sneaking treats out of the kitchen pantry (for me, that was a mixture of powdered milk and sugar designed to leave the tongue cleft to the roof of my mouth, and occasionally adding chocolaty granules of Milo to the mixture that left me in a culinary ecstasy). Upon discovering these precious items were missing, Mommy would bellow, "Who took the milk and sugar?"

I dared not tell the truth, knowing I would surely be punished by divulging my theft. So, I learned to keep silent unless discovered by the straying bits of milk at the corners of my mouth.

I also learned to be silent in telling the truth after seeing other siblings get a spanking when they were honest. So, I learned that truth was not something to rejoice in. As I continued in life, I unconsciously would tell lies about what I felt or who I was so that I could "fit in" and be acceptable to what other people wanted me to be.

As a child, without the emotional maturity of what I was doing, the lies became my reality, and I did not know that I did not know the truth. Yes, I learned in Sunday School that "Thou shall not lie" and "liars would be cast into the lake of fire;" that placed even more fear in me, so I told the truth the best I knew how to while trying to avoid punishment.

265

As I matured and my spiritual life developed, I grew into this woman who prided herself on honesty, trying to be my most authentic self but still unaware that some of the truths I believed and adhered to were lies that became my reality. Once I faced the truth of infidelity in my marriage, I was forced to take a long, hard look at myself, not at my ex-husband (that was his work to do), but at myself.

I remember the pain of that journey; I asked God to reveal the truth to me. At that time, I believed the revealed truth would be about everything my ex-spouse was doing wrong. Still, God, in His magnificent grace and wisdom, also began revealing the Truth to me, about me, about Him and me. I asked God to do this deep work in my life and heart because I told Him to show me why I made the poor decisions I did with relationships. I was finally ready to face the Truth, not as I wished things to be.

I was prepared to face the Light and come out from behind the shadows of the self-imposed lies I used to survive, no matter how painful that would be.

If I were going to be in pain, I preferred the pain of transformation to that of the painful self-defeating decisions that had taken me around the same fruitless mountain for so many years without any true emotional healing. That began the journey and the process of my emotional healing and the strengthening of my spiritual relationship.

There cannot be any repair of our emotional, spiritual, or physical woundedness without Truth. I believe that there are thousands, if not millions, who, like me, have a fear of the Truth, who may not even know what Truth looks like, having embraced falsity because it has helped them to have some semblance of sanity to survive the world in which they live.

For those who have become aware of this and want to walk this journey of unconditional love, I encourage you to first embrace the Truth of Who God is, who you are, and your earthly and eternal destination.

I am still learning, and I can testify that the scripture in **John 8:32** that says, "You shall know the Truth and the Truth shall set you free," is true. Lies place shackles on us, our minds, souls, and bodies. The more Truth you know, believe, and embrace, the more those shackles fall to the ground and set you free.

Today, I can say Love rejoices in the truth; even when that truth may hurt at first, because I know it is coming from a place of God's unconditional love. So it will always be for my good and His glory. I am still learning to tell the truth about myself and how I feel in the moment, and I am doing so with love. Learning to tell the truth about myself (without self-condemnation) helps me be more transparent so I can be seen and accepted for who I truly am.

I no longer have to, nor want to hide behind a false persona that I may believe is acceptable to others. God created us with our special DNA and fingerprints that make us unique and special to Him, if not to others.

He broke each mold when he created each one of us. Truth is the key that frees us to be our authentic selves. God's Truth is the key to our true identity.

As we become more truthful with God and ourselves, we can tell the truth to our neighbors (those we have relationships with or encounter). **Ephesians 4:25** encourages us to "Reject ALL falsehood (whether lying, defrauding, telling half-truths, spreading rumors, any such as these), SPEAK TRUTH EACH ONE WITH HIS NEIGHBOR, for we are all parts of one another."

Before king David could conquer the giant, he had to walk and believe the truth about whose he was and who he was. Some want others to validate or make them believe something about who they are when they do not believe that about themselves.

David could not depend on external validation to determine who he was. Not even his father or brothers could tell who he really was.

Look at the events recorded in the Bible, such as when the Lord told the prophet Samuel to anoint the next king of Israel since He had rejected Saul. "You shall invite Jesse to the sacrifice, and I will show you what you shall do [after that], and you shall anoint for Me the one whom I designate." **1 Samuel 16:3.**

"So it happened when they had come, he looked at Eliab [the eldest son] and thought, 'Surely the Lord's anointed is before Him.' But the Lord told Samuel, 'Do not look at his appearance or the height of his stature because I have rejected him.' For the Lord sees not as man sees; for man looks at the outward appearance, but the Lord looks at the heart." **1 Samuel 16:6-7.** Jesse had seven of his sons pass before Samuel. But Samuel told Jesse, "The Lord has not chosen [any of] these." Then Samuel said to Jesse, "Are all your sons here?" Jesse replied, "There is still one left, the youngest; he is tending the sheep." Samuel told Jesse, "Send word and bring him because we will not sit down [to eat the sacrificial meal] until he comes here." **1 Samuel 16:10-11.**

"So, Jesse sent word and brought him in. Now, he had a ruddy complexion, beautiful eyes, and a handsome appearance. The Lord said [to Samuel], 'Arise, anoint him; for this is he.' Then Samuel took the horn of oil and anointed David in the presence of his brothers. The Spirit of the Lord came mightily upon David from that day forward. And Samuel arose and went to Ramah." **1 Samuel 16:12-13.**

So many of us will have to fight through the lies we have been told that we are not good enough. We learned that mainly from the families who raised us. It was not easy since this was the first introduction to self, how those around you saw you and told you who you were.

It became your identity.

But just as David the shepherd boy spent countless hours and years communing, listening, and believing who his true heavenly Father said he was, so too, your faith and belief in who you were created to be will come by hearing repeatedly the Word of God.

This is true and will be the same for anyone who wants to be victorious over the giants within and the ones we face without.

Here are some truths about who God says you are. "But without faith, it is impossible to [walk with God and] please Him, for whoever comes [near] to God must [necessarily] believe that God exists and that He rewards those who [earnestly and diligently] seek Him." **Hebrews 11:6** First, believe God exists as the Creator and Ruler of all things, especially you, His beloved creation.

- Created in God's Image (Imago Dei)

Genesis 1:26-27: Humans are created in the image and likeness of God, which imparts inherent value, dignity, and purpose to every individual. Being made in God's image means we are reflections of His character and are appointed stewards of the earth. **Psalm 139:13-14**: "For you created my inmost being; you knit me together in my mother's womb. I praise you because I am fearfully and wonderfully made."

This suggests that God values each person as a unique creation.

- I am, you are, a child of God

John 1:12-13, Romans 8:14-17: Those who believe in (adhere to, trust in, and rely on) Jesus and accept Him are given the right (the authority, the privilege) to become children of God, (born not of natural conception, nor the will of physical impulses, the will of man, but of God, a supernatural rebirth, spiritually transformed, renewed, sanctified) adopted into His family.

This relationship is marked by intimacy, love, and inheritance.

- When we become God's beloved children, we become Temples of His Holy Spirit. **1 Corinthians 6:19-20**: For believers, our bodies are considered temples of the Holy Spirit, signifying that God dwells within and sanctifies them. This indicates a high level of honor and responsibility.

• God calls us a Priesthood of Believers

1 Peter 2:9: We are described as, "A chosen race, a royal priesthood, a consecrated nation, a special people for God's possession, called to proclaim God's excellent and wonderful deeds and virtues, who called us out of darkness into His marvelous Light." This suggests a direct and active role in worship and service. This active role is purposed for whatever part of the world we live in. We are called to bear witness to the goodness of God to our tribe, people, and sphere of influence.

• Created for Good Works

Ephesians 2:10: "We are God's handiwork (His workmanship, His masterwork, a work of art), created in Christ Jesus, ready to be used to do good works, which God prepared in advance for us to do, walking the paths which He set for us, so we would live the good life which He prearranged and made ready for us." This suggests that humans have a purposeful role in God's plan.

The idea that each person was created with a unique purpose indicates that his/her creation was intentional. I love that the Creator of all the universe, the galaxies and stars, the earth above and the earth beneath, the land and the seas, has considered to make us His most marvelous handiwork, workmanship, work of art. Picasso has nothing on us. This implies that God thoughtfully crafted everyone with specific talents, abilities, and a distinct role to play in the world.

We are not created to exist and then die into nothingness. Each human being is designed with a purpose, and our lives have meaning. The beautiful journey with God is discovering what that is and walking in that calling.

If each person has a unique purpose, it indicates that every individual has something important to contribute that no one else can exactly replicate. This reinforces the idea that each person is valuable because they fulfill a part of God's overall plan that only they can achieve.

In a world where everyone has a distinct purpose, the variety of skills, perspectives, and talents enriches the human experience. The diversity reflects God's creative nature and demonstrates His value in multifaceted expressions. One of my favorite scriptures that has enhanced my relationship with Christ is my belief in **Jeremiah 29:11,** "'For I know the plans I have for you,' declares the LORD, 'plans to prosper you and not to harm you, plans to give you hope and a future.'" This spoke to me when I felt like Sofia in the movie, "The Color Purple," as she said, "All my life I had to fight…." This scripture sank deep within me that God was not going to and, in fact, had no intention of hurting me.

I did not have to fight with Him because He had great plans for me, plans to prosper and not harm me, plans to give me hope (which I desperately needed), and a future.

I had been fighting everyone for so long, fighting for the right to be heard, seen, and loved.

I was fighting my fears within and the fears without. It took me years to realize that I had been living in survival mode, always uptight, always tense, all ready to set it off, triggered quickly and like a walking, ticking time bomb. The tenderness and love the Lord showed me through this scripture began to dissolve the protective wall in my heart and soul that kept people out but left me imprisoned within. He showed me that not only was I loved but that I was seen.

I was created for a plan and purpose, and those were for good and not for evil. That plan included prospering, but most importantly, He would not harm/hurt me. I could trust Him. God loves, sees, and accepts me, which is evident in His plan for me and each person.

- Heirs with Christ

Romans 8:17, Galatians 4:7: As children of God, we are no longer like slaves but now sons and daughters and, as such, co-heirs with Christ.

Because believers share in God's spiritual blessings, they are promised an eternal inheritance, indicating the lasting bond and reward in their relationship with God.

- New Creation

This is so exciting. God makes us new when we accept this marvelous Love He bestows on us, and believe in Christ's birth, death, resurrection, and finished work of the Cross.

Some of us do not believe that because we keep dragging around the baggage of our old life, our old way of thinking. God loves us so much that He continually seeks to renew our minds to the Truth.

2 Corinthians 5:17, Galatians 6:15: In Christ, believers become new creations, leaving behind the old life of sin and embracing a new life transformed by God's power because spiritual awakening brings new life.

- Ambassadors for Christ

2 Corinthians 5:20: Believers are called to be ambassadors for Christ, meaning they are representatives of His kingdom and messengers of reconciliation to the world. We can go on and on about the Truths in the Word of God that can revolutionize our lives. However, I will leave it here so you can have the fantastic delight of discovering some of these Truths yourself.

Let us examine some of the effects being untruthful can have on our and others' lives. Dishonesty harms individuals, relationships, families, and society.

Effects on Individuals

1. **Trust Erosion**

When individuals lie, they damage the trust others have in them, and there is also an erosion of trust in oneself.

How devasting it must be not to be able to trust the person you see in the mirror. I do not believe we have fully considered the internal damage this does to the individual. I have heard numerous stories of the self-loathing people feel when they think they have let themselves down, time and time again. When we begin to be able to trust ourselves and our decisions and keep our word to the one who looks back at us in the mirror, there is an exhilaration and sense of freedom that is indescribable. It also is a motivator to continue emotional growth and maturity. You begin trusting, loving, and respecting the man or woman looking back at you in the mirror because you are looking at a transparent person. Truth sets you free.

2. Stress

Maintaining lies may lead to stress and anxiety, as individuals must remember the details of their falsehoods to avoid being caught. I read a quote some time ago that said you never have to remember what you said when you tell the truth. When a person tells a lie, it can trigger a stress response.

The brain recognizes the risk of getting caught, which activates the sympathetic nervous system, which can increase heart rate, blood pressure, and respiration rate as the body prepares for a 'fight or flight' response. Lying also increases cognitive load as the brain must work harder to fabricate a story, keep track of the lie, and suppress the truth, thus leading to decreased cognitive efficiency in other tasks and increased mental fatigue.

I once interacted with an individual (that I later discovered) who lied constantly and consistently.

Whenever I came close to a lie being exposed, that individual would shut down and suddenly become tired and sleep for hours. Now, it can also be an act of avoidance, but I can look back now and see elements of fear and mental fatigue.

Over time, the brain may become structured to facilitate dishonesty more readily, affecting behavior patterns and possibly even moral judgments.

3. Hormonal Fluctuations

Stress hormones such as cortisol may be released in greater quantities when lying, which, if chronic, can affect various bodily functions and potentially contribute to health issues like weakened immune responses and metabolic changes.

4. Psychological Discomfort

The tension between maintaining a lie and a person's desire or need to be truthful can cause psychological discomfort, often called cognitive dissonance.

This disharmony can manifest as physical symptoms such as headaches, nausea, or feelings of unease.

5. Behavioral Signs

While the physiological consequences might not always be outwardly visible, the body can exhibit behavioral signs of lying, such as fidgeting, averted eye contact, excessive blinking, or other nervous gestures.

6. The Long-Term Health Effects

Prolonged exposure to stress caused by living a dishonest life can contribute to long-term health issues such as anxiety, depression, heart problems, and more.

7. Impact on Relationships

Though not strictly a physiological effect, the strain of dishonesty on personal and professional relationships can lead to social stress, which may worsen physiological symptoms.

It should be noted that some become desensitized to these responses over time, mainly if they engage in dishonest behavior frequently. Nevertheless, the physiological impacts of dishonesty highlight the not-so-apparent toll that lying can take on an individual's health and well-being.

Being caught in a lie can harm a person's reputation, affecting future opportunities and social standing. Then there is the guilt and shame.

Lying can elicit feelings of guilt and shame, potentially causing psychological stress and impacting mental health. It can also be habit-forming. Regular dishonesty can become a habit, making it easier to lie in the future and more challenging to maintain integrity.

Even the "little white lies" can desensitize us to truth-telling, leading to "bigger lies" until we feel no guilt or shame, justifying this dangerous habit until something catastrophic happens.

<u>Effects on Families</u>

1. **Trust Issues**. Dishonesty within a family can lead to deep-seated trust issues, causing members to question one another's actions and intentions.

2. **Emotional Distance**. Family members may become emotionally detached to protect themselves from the hurt that lies and betrayal cause.

3. **Role Modeling**. Parents who lie set a poor precedent for their children, who may mimic this behavior, believing it is an acceptable way to navigate life situations.

There is a saying that children do not do as they are told; they do what they see. Can you imagine the negative impact this has on them?

We scold or chastise children when we catch them in a lie, but we admonish them to tell the bill collector we are not home when they call or knock at the door.

4. **Conflict**. Lies can lead to arguments and ongoing conflict as the truth eventually surfaces, risking long-term relationships.

Effects on Society

1. **Social Mistrust**. Widespread dishonesty can create an atmosphere of general mistrust, where people doubt the integrity of others.

2. **Economic Impact**. Dishonesty, like fraud or corruption, has a direct negative impact on the economy, increasing costs for everyone.

3. **Injustice**. Lies can lead to false accusations and wrongful convictions, disrupting the lives of innocent people and undermining the justice system.

4. **Political Disenfranchisement**. Political dishonesty can lead to citizen apathy and disengagement, weakening democratic processes and governance.

Proverbs 11:3 says, "The integrity and moral courage of the upright will guide them, but the crookedness of the treacherous will destroy them." Organizations and governments' lack of integrity can destabilize their moral and economic potential.

5. **Cultural Shift**. Pervasive dishonesty can shift cultural norms, where dishonest behavior becomes normalized, further entrenching deceitful practices across various areas of society.

Unfortunately, this is accepted and glamorized in many cultures worldwide. It can be seen in our movies and on social media platforms.

But **Zechariah 8:16** says, "These are the things which you should do; speak the truth with one another: judge with truth and pronounce the judgment that brings peace at your gates." These are the places of our governments, laws, and judicial systems.

Lying and dishonesty fundamentally threaten the fabric of trust necessary for cooperative and harmonious relations at all levels of interaction.

While occasional dishonesty might seem trivial, its cumulative effect can substantially harm personal relations, societal institutions, and overall quality of life.

An important fact to remember and think about is that lying and being dishonest are rooted in fear. Such misdeeds separate and place a veil between our relationship with God and others. God invites us to receive His love because, in His love, there is no fear, only Truth and transparency where we are seen and accepted for who we are (flaws and all).

Walking in His Truth is walking in Light and no longer in darkness. Light dispels darkness. Light allows us to walk in awareness and not blindly endure life's journey. Light illuminates. Things that confused us before are now clear to our understanding. Truth is Light, and that sets us free. To rejoice in the Truth, it is essential to learn to tell the truth in every aspect of our lives. Love rejoices in the truth.

When we do not know or choose not to believe the Truth of God's Word, it robs us of hope, faith, peace, and joy. Lies are always shrouded in darkness, even darkness that presents itself as light. So, where do lies come from? Let us go back to the beginning.

Before Satan, formerly Lucifer, a worship leader in heaven, was cast out of heaven, he conceived lies (that presented as truth) to 1/3 of the angels of heaven. He led them in a rebellion against God, His Majesty, and the throne of heaven. "How you have fallen from heaven, O star of the morning [light-bringer], son of the dawn!

You have been cut down to the ground, you who have weakened the nations [king of Babylon]!" **Isaiah 14:12.** "But you said in your heart, 'I will ascend to heaven; I will raise my throne above the stars of God; I will sit on the mount of assembly in the remote parts of the north.'" **Isaiah 14:13.**

This is what God's Word says about the true character and nature of Satan, as Jesus was admonishing those who did not believe in Him and challenged Who He was/is. In **John 8:44**, Jesus said to them, "You are of your father the devil, and it is your will to practice the desires (which are characteristic) of your father.

Satan was a murderer from the beginning and does not stand in the truth because there is no truth in him. He speaks what is natural to him when he lies, for he is a liar and the father of lies (and half-truths)."

Satan is not capable of being truthful and yet disguises himself as an angel of light and has deceived many. Then he (Satan) went to the first man and woman, Adam and Eve, and did the same thing. He took some truth mixed with lies and deceived them into rebelling against God's word.

This is why it is imperative we continually bathe our minds in the Truth and Light of God's Word so that we, too, will not be deceived by Satan's lies.

So many have fallen prey to his deception, and we see the evil effects in our world. Many of the enemy's deception is subtle and can seem convincing if you do not know the Truth. Some say truth is relative, and if so, everyone can do what seems correct or truthful to them in their own eyes (look at the results of those choices in our world today).

After His resurrection and before He ascended to heaven, Jesus spent time with His disciples, comforting them about His departure and letting them know that not only would He leave His Holy Spirit to be with them always, but that He was going before them to prepare a place for them so that where He is, they will also be.

Probably frightened, Thomas asked Jesus how they would know how to come to Him. Jesus responded in **John 14:6** by saying to him, "I am the (only) Way (to God) and the (real) Truth and the (real) Life; no one comes to the Father but through Me."

<u>**Reflection**</u>:

Maybe you are asking the same questions.

There are so many deceptions in our world today that you do not know what to believe; you feel like you have lost your way and do not know which path to choose or what road to travel.

I believe in my heart that you want the right path; you want to choose the right road because you have traveled down many other roads that have only resulted in dead ends or self-destruction. This is your crossroads and only you can choose. Just remember that Satan is a deceiver. He knows how to seduce us.

Most of the time, he will not present you with a blatant lie but ones disguised to look like truths or light. If we do not know and stand on what God has said, Satan will lead us astray and down a destructive path. Those who are deceived follow a deceptive lie since Satan comes only to steal, kill, and destroy.

No matter how sweet and enticing the lie appears, it will eventually lead to destruction of your life and those around you. The devil's destiny is already sealed, and he wants to take as many of God's beloved creations with him.

The angel "Opened the bottomless pit, and smoke like the smoke of a great furnace flowed out of the pit; and the sun and the atmosphere were darkened by the smoke from the pit" **Revelation 9:2.**

"And war broke out in heaven, Michael [the archangel] and his angels waging war with the dragon.

The dragon and his angels fought, but they were not strong enough and did not prevail, and there was no longer a place found for them in heaven.

And the great dragon was thrown down, the age-old serpent who is called the devil and Satan, he who continually deceives and seduces the entire inhabited world; he was thrown down to the earth, and his angels were thrown down with him" **Revelation 12:7-9.**

The truth is he hates you and me because we were and are created in God's image and likeness.

Consider your attitude toward honesty and truthfulness. Do you find joy in speaking the truth, even when it may be difficult or uncomfortable?

To speak and rejoice in the Truth, we must first know the Truth and the One who is the Truth.

Debra Enile Armand

Prayer:

Heavenly Father, thank You for revealing Yourself as the Source of Truth. Please help me to embrace and celebrate truth in every aspect of my life. Give me the courage and wisdom to speak the truth in love, even when challenging. You are the Truth, and Your Truth will set me free from the enslavement and entanglements of this world. Your Truth brings Light to illuminate every dark and deceptive ploy of the enemy disguised to entrap and enslave me. As I walk in Your Truth, I believe You will continue to guide and protect me along life's journey. I desire to be truthful with You, myself, and others.

May my words and actions always align with Your Truth.

In Jesus' Name, Amen.

Reflection/Note-taking

_____

_____

_____

_____

_____

Reflection/Note-taking

_____

_____

_____

_____

_____

Day 30

God's Unconditional Love

Scripture: **1 Corinthians 13:13:** "And now there remain: faith (abiding trust in God and His Promises), hope (confident expectation of eternal salvation), love (unselfish love for others growing out of God's love for me), these three (the choices of graces); but the greatest of these is love."

Devotional:

This is a space to write about your experiences and lessons learned through this journey. Love, God's unconditional love, is the foundation for every aspect of life.

Be blessed, beloved.

Conclusion

Love, unconditional love is a decision. This has profoundly mind-boggled me throughout the writing of this devotional journey. But I felt it explode within me one crisp wintry desert morning as I made a keto savory Dutch Baby Bread and meditated on **1 Corinthian 13:13:** "And now there remain: faith (abiding trust in God and His promises), hope (confident expectation of eternal salvation), love (unselfish love for others growing out of God's love for me), these three (the choicest graces); but the greatest of these is love." Unconditional love solves envy, jealousy, pride, rudeness, self-seeking, anger, unforgiveness, and all the destruction that comes with these traits. I have tried my best to describe a microscopic portion of this incredible journey with God, my Father, Savior, and Lord, Jesus Christ, by the power of His Holy Spirit living in me.

I still fall short of what I know is His unending, unfailing love for you and me (for now, I only know in part, just fragments, but one day, as I and we come face to face with Him, we will fully know as He fully knows us). But one of the most healing truths I have come to believe, undyingly, is that love is a path to choose, founded and paved by God.

With God's amazing love for us poured out daily, we still must choose to receive this. We delay choosing God's therapeutic love due to the emotional trauma we endured during our formative years from individuals who experienced similar traumas in their early years. We cannot give what we do not have, and some have undeservingly experienced trauma that no human being should go through. But because you are still here on earth, still standing, still reading these pages, still intensely yearning for what is described here, it means that God is still reaching out to you.

Your last chapter can be completely different from your first page. You did not choose the timing of your birth, the family you were born into, or what you have been through, but now, you do have a choice as to how you will journey through the rest of your life. That is your power to choose. Choose love instead of fear. Choose love instead of hate, unforgiveness, bitterness, or pride.

Everyone has the power of choice. You must realize that you can pour unconditional love into others, but unless they choose to receive it, it will be useless to them. This was particularly powerful to me as God's Holy Spirit impressed upon me that not only is God love and His love permeates the portals of heaven, but Lucifer abided in that environment and still chose to rebel against God, in seeking and wanting all the adoration for himself (selfish pride). Satan wants unconditional love, not to give out but to hoard for his gain.

He is an imposter, a liar, the father of lies, a plagiarizer, and a hater of all the good that God has created. **Genesis 3:1, Revelation 12:7-9, Ezekiel 28:12-18.** The angels in heaven are not mindless robotic beings. God has given them, created beings like us, the power to choose His love or not. **Isaiah 14:12-14. Lucifer made a choice to reject God's love.** The created wanted to become the Creator, and thus, his fall and his coming destiny. You and I have choices every moment of every day. I choose God's love and pray that you open your hearts to do the same. Your life will never be the same.

Reflection/Note-taking

_____

_____

_____

_____

_____

Reflection/Note-taking

_____

_____

_____

_____

_____

_____

www.ingramcontent.com/pod-product-compliance
Lightning Source LLC
Chambersburg PA
CBHW051507120626
46551CB00012B/811